All About Serengeti: A Kid's Guide to Africa's Most Famous Wildlife Destination

Educational Books For Kids, Volume 33

Shah Rukh

Published by Shah Rukh, 2024.

ALL ABOUT SERENGETI: A KID'S GUIDE TO AFRICA'S MOST FAMOUS WILDLIFE DESTINATION

First edition. October 18, 2024.

Copyright © 2024 Shah Rukh.

ISBN: 979-8227956422

Written by Shah Rukh.

Table of Contents

Prologue

Welcome to the wild and wonderful world of the Serengeti! Stretching across Tanzania and Kenya, the Serengeti is one of the most incredible places on Earth, filled with amazing animals, fascinating landscapes, and the heart-pounding adventures of the wild. From the thundering hooves of millions of wildebeest on their Great Migration to the roar of lions in the golden grass, every corner of the Serengeti is packed with life and excitement.

In this book, we'll take you on an unforgettable journey through Africa's most famous wildlife destination. You'll meet towering giraffes, speedy cheetahs, and mighty elephants, and discover the unique roles each animal plays in the circle of life. Along the way, you'll also learn about the Maasai people who have lived here for centuries, protecting and respecting this incredible environment.

Get ready to explore the open savannas, cross flowing rivers, and learn how this wild paradise stays in balance through changing seasons and natural wonders. Whether you're a young adventurer or just love nature, the Serengeti is waiting to share its secrets with you!

Chapter 1: Exploring the Vast Plains of the Serengeti

Imagine stepping into a world that seems to stretch on forever, where the land meets the sky in a vast sea of golden grass, and herds of animals move as far as the eye can see. This is the Serengeti, one of the most famous and incredible places on Earth. The Serengeti is a gigantic plain located in East Africa, mostly in Tanzania, but it also stretches into parts of Kenya. Its name comes from the Maasai language, and it means "endless plains." And that's exactly what the Serengeti feels like—an endless land filled with life, adventure, and surprises.

The Serengeti's plains are covered with tall grasses that sway in the breeze. These grasses provide food and shelter for countless animals, both big and small. As you explore these vast plains, you might spot some of the most well-known animals in the world. Lions, often called the kings of the jungle, roam the land in search of food. They are majestic creatures with powerful roars that can be heard from miles away. Sometimes, you can see them lounging under the shade of a tree, waiting for the cooler evening to begin their hunt.

Nearby, you might notice zebras, their black-and-white stripes standing out against the golden grass. These stripes might look pretty to us, but they help the zebras blend in with their surroundings and confuse predators like lions and hyenas. Herds of wildebeest, one of the most famous animals of the Serengeti, graze across the plains. These large, shaggy creatures are always on the move, traveling hundreds of miles each year during the Great Migration, a journey that brings millions of wildebeest, zebras, and other animals across the Serengeti in search of fresh grass and water.

One of the most amazing things about the Serengeti is how so many different types of animals live together. You can see elephants, the largest land animals in the world, wandering in groups called herds.

These gentle giants use their trunks to grab leaves from trees and to drink water from rivers and lakes. Their enormous size helps protect them from most predators, but they still rely on each other to stay safe. Giraffes, the tallest animals on Earth, are also a common sight in the Serengeti. Their long necks allow them to reach leaves high up in the trees that other animals can't get to, giving them a special place in the ecosystem.

The Serengeti is also home to some of the fastest animals in the world. Cheetahs, known for their incredible speed, can sprint across the plains at lightning speed, chasing down gazelles and other small animals. Watching a cheetah run is like seeing nature's version of a race car—quick, sleek, and unstoppable. But not all animals in the Serengeti are as large as lions or as fast as cheetahs. There are also smaller creatures, like meerkats, who live in tunnels beneath the ground, and warthogs, which can often be seen running with their tails straight up in the air. Each of these animals plays a special role in the Serengeti's ecosystem, and together they create a balance that has existed for thousands of years.

The sky over the Serengeti is as impressive as the land below. During the day, the sun shines brightly, casting a golden glow over the plains. The sky is often a brilliant blue, dotted with fluffy white clouds. As the day goes on, the sky changes, turning shades of pink, orange, and purple as the sun sets. And when night falls, the Serengeti is covered by a blanket of stars, more stars than you could ever count. It's so dark and clear that you can see the Milky Way, our galaxy, stretching across the sky. At night, the sounds of the Serengeti come alive, with animals like hyenas and jackals calling out to one another in the darkness.

Water is very important in the Serengeti, and many of the animals depend on rivers and waterholes to survive. The Seronera River is one of the main water sources in the Serengeti. Along its banks, you can see animals gathering to drink, from graceful antelopes to massive hippos. Crocodiles lurk in the water, waiting for an opportunity to catch their next meal. These rivers are lifelines for the Serengeti's creatures, especially during the dry season when water is harder to find.

But the Serengeti isn't just about the animals. It's also about the people who live there and have been part of its history for thousands of years. The Maasai people, known for their colorful clothes and unique traditions, have lived on the Serengeti's plains for generations. They are skilled cattle herders and live in harmony with the wildlife, respecting the animals and the land that provides for them. The Maasai have a deep connection to the Serengeti, and they play an important role in preserving this incredible place for future generations.

One of the most famous events in the Serengeti is the Great Migration, a natural wonder that happens every year. During the migration, millions of animals travel across the Serengeti and into the neighboring Maasai Mara in Kenya. This journey is one of the largest and most impressive movements of animals in the world. It's a dangerous trip, with predators like lions, cheetahs, and crocodiles waiting for their chance to hunt. But for the wildebeest, zebras, and other animals, the migration is a necessary part of survival, as they search for new grass and water.

The Serengeti is also an important place for conservation. Many of the animals that live there, like elephants and rhinos, are endangered, meaning their populations are at risk of disappearing. Conservationists and park rangers work hard to protect these animals from poachers, people who illegally hunt animals for their horns, tusks, or skins. Thanks to their efforts, the Serengeti remains one of the best places in the world to see wildlife in its natural habitat.

Exploring the vast plains of the Serengeti is like stepping into a living, breathing world full of adventure and discovery. Every corner of the Serengeti has something new to offer, whether it's spotting a lion stalking its prey, watching the graceful movements of a giraffe as it nibbles on leaves, or listening to the sounds of the savannah at night.

The Serengeti is not just a place; it's an experience that stays with you forever, reminding you of the beauty, power, and wonder of nature.

Chapter 2: The Great Migration Adventure

The Great Migration is one of the most incredible adventures on Earth, a natural wonder that happens every year in the vast plains of the Serengeti and the Maasai Mara in East Africa. It's a journey like no other, where millions of animals—mainly wildebeest, but also zebras and gazelles—embark on an epic quest across the land. They travel hundreds of miles, facing danger at every turn, all in search of fresh grass and water. Imagine an ocean of animals moving together, a sea of life that stretches as far as the eye can see. This is the Great Migration, and it's one of the most exciting things you could ever witness.

The story of the Great Migration begins with the changing seasons. The Serengeti, which is where the journey starts, is a huge grassland that experiences both rainy and dry seasons. When the rains come, the grass grows tall and green, and the animals have plenty to eat. But when the dry season arrives, the grass starts to wither, and the waterholes dry up. The animals, especially the wildebeest, know that they have to move to survive. They begin their journey north, following the rains and the promise of fresh, green grass.

The wildebeest, also called gnus, are the stars of the Great Migration. These large, shaggy creatures might not look very fast or strong, but they are amazing travelers. There are over 1.5 million wildebeest that take part in the migration every year. Along with them are hundreds of thousands of zebras and gazelles, which move together in a massive herd. It's like the ultimate road trip for animals, but instead of cars, there are hooves, and instead of roads, there are grassy plains and rivers.

The journey is not easy. The animals have to cross rivers, face predators, and deal with exhaustion and hunger. One of the most dangerous parts of the migration is crossing the Mara River. The Mara

River is full of fast-moving water and even more dangerous, it's home to huge Nile crocodiles. These crocodiles have been waiting all year for this moment. As the wildebeest approach the river, the crocodiles lurk just beneath the surface, waiting for their chance to strike. The wildebeest have to gather their courage and plunge into the river, swimming as fast as they can to reach the other side. It's a heart-pounding scene, with wildebeest leaping into the water, some making it safely across, while others fall victim to the hungry crocs.

But the Mara River isn't the only challenge the animals face. The plains of the Serengeti and the Maasai Mara are home to many predators, and during the migration, they have a feast of opportunities. Lions, cheetahs, leopards, and hyenas all follow the migrating herds, looking for a chance to hunt. For the wildebeest, zebras, and gazelles, every day is a test of survival. They have to stay alert, always watching for predators hiding in the tall grass. Sometimes, you might see a lioness stalking through the grass, getting closer and closer to an unsuspecting wildebeest. When the moment is right, she charges, and the chase begins. Only the fastest and strongest animals escape, but for the lions and other predators, the migration is a time of plenty.

As the herds move north, they travel through different parts of the Serengeti and the Maasai Mara, each with its own challenges and rewards. In some areas, the grass is tall and green, offering the animals plenty to eat. But in other places, the grass has been eaten down to the roots, and the animals have to keep moving to find fresh food. Sometimes, the herds split up, with smaller groups going in different directions, but they always come back together as they continue their journey.

One of the most amazing things about the Great Migration is that it never really stops. Even when the animals reach the Maasai Mara and find fresh grass, they don't stay there forever. After a few months, the rains begin to fall again in the Serengeti, and the grass grows back. So, the animals turn around and head back south, retracing their steps and starting the whole adventure over again. It's a never-ending cycle, driven by the rains and the changing seasons. The animals are always on the move, always looking for the next place to eat and drink.

The Great Migration isn't just a test of survival for the animals; it's also a reminder of how connected everything in nature is. The wildebeest and other herbivores follow the rains because they need the grass to survive. But without these migrating animals, the predators like lions and cheetahs would have a much harder time finding food. And the plants themselves benefit from the migration, too. As the animals move across the land, they spread seeds and fertilize the soil with their droppings, helping the grass to grow back after they've passed through. It's a beautiful example of how all living things depend on one another to survive.

For the Maasai people, who live in the regions around the Serengeti and Maasai Mara, the migration is an important part of their culture and way of life. The Maasai are cattle herders, and they have lived in harmony with the land and the wildlife for generations. They understand the importance of the migration and the need to protect the animals and the environment. Today, the Maasai work alongside conservationists to make sure that the migration can continue for many years to come. They help protect the animals from poachers and work to preserve the land where the animals travel.

Tourists from all over the world come to see the Great Migration. It's one of the most popular wildlife events in the world, and for good reason. Seeing millions of animals on the move, hearing the thunder of their hooves as they run across the plains, and watching the dramatic river crossings is something that leaves people in awe. The Great Migration is like a real-life adventure movie, filled with excitement, danger, and beauty. Many people travel to the Serengeti and the Maasai Mara to witness this incredible event, and it has become an important part of tourism in East Africa.

Conservation efforts are a big part of the Great Migration, too. Over the years, people have worked hard to protect the Serengeti and the animals that live there. National parks have been created to give the animals a safe place to live and migrate without being disturbed by human activities. Rangers and conservationists patrol the land to stop illegal hunting and to make sure that the migration can continue. It's important to protect this natural wonder because without the migration, the Serengeti and the Maasai Mara would be very different places. The balance of nature would be thrown off, and many of the animals that rely on the migration could be in danger.

The Great Migration is a powerful reminder of the beauty and power of nature. It shows us how animals can work together to survive in a challenging world, and how they can overcome incredible obstacles, from predators to dangerous river crossings. The sight of millions of wildebeest, zebras, and gazelles moving together across the land is something that stays with you forever. It's a story of survival, adventure, and the never-ending search for food and water in a world where nature is always changing. For the animals of the Serengeti and the Maasai Mara, the migration is life itself, and for those lucky enough to witness it, it's an unforgettable experience.

The Great Migration adventure is a journey that never ends. Every year, the cycle begins again, with the animals following the rains, crossing rivers, facing predators, and moving through one of the most stunning landscapes on Earth. It's a natural wonder that has been happening for thousands of years, and with continued efforts to protect the land and the animals, it's a journey that will hopefully continue for many more.

Chapter 3: Meet the Big Five of the Serengeti

The Serengeti is one of the most famous places in the world for wildlife, and it's home to some of the most incredible animals you can imagine. Among all the creatures that roam its vast plains, none are more legendary than the "Big Five." The Big Five refers to five of the most impressive and powerful animals that live in Africa: the lion, the leopard, the elephant, the buffalo, and the rhinoceros. These animals got their name not because of their size, but because they were considered the most difficult to hunt by big-game hunters in the past. Today, instead of hunting these majestic animals, people from all over the world come to see them in the wild, hoping to catch a glimpse of these magnificent creatures in their natural habitat.

Let's start by meeting the king of the Big Five—the lion. The lion is known as the "king of the jungle," even though it doesn't live in the jungle. Instead, it thrives in the grasslands and savannahs of the Serengeti. Lions are powerful, social animals, and they live in groups called prides. A pride can include up to 30 lions, usually led by a dominant male. The male lions are easy to recognize because of their thick, flowing manes, which make them look even more majestic. These manes can be dark brown, black, or golden, and they serve as a sign of strength. The bigger and darker a lion's mane, the more intimidating he is to other lions.

Lions are expert hunters, and they usually hunt in groups. It's the females who do most of the hunting, while the males protect the pride. Together, the females work as a team, using their speed and strength to bring down prey like zebras, antelopes, and wildebeest. Once they catch their meal, the males join in to eat first, followed by the rest of the pride. Lions are known for their loud roars, which can be heard up to five miles away. These roars help them communicate with each other, mark their territory, and scare off rivals.

Next up is the leopard, another member of the Big Five. Leopards are known for their grace and stealth. Unlike lions, which live in groups, leopards are solitary creatures. They prefer to live and hunt alone, which makes them harder to spot in the wild. But when you do see one, it's a breathtaking sight. Leopards have beautiful golden coats with dark spots called rosettes. These spots help them blend into the surrounding trees and grass, making it easier for them to stalk their prey.

Leopards are incredible climbers, and they often drag their prey up into the trees to keep it safe from other predators like lions and hyenas. They can leap great distances and are incredibly strong for their size. Even though they're smaller than lions, leopards are fierce hunters, taking down animals much larger than themselves, such as antelope and wildebeest. They hunt at night, using their excellent vision to see in the dark. Because they are so good at hiding, leopards are considered the most elusive of the Big Five, and spotting one in the wild is a rare and special treat.

Now let's talk about the African elephant, the largest land animal in the world and a true giant of the Serengeti. Elephants are known for their incredible size, intelligence, and gentle nature. Adult elephants can weigh as much as 14,000 pounds and stand up to 13 feet tall at the shoulder. They have massive ears that help them stay cool in the hot African sun and long trunks that they use for all sorts of things, from picking up food to spraying water on themselves.

Elephants are highly social animals, living in groups called herds. These herds are led by a matriarch, an older, experienced female who guides the group. Elephants are known for their strong family bonds, and they take care of each other in times of need. For example, if a young elephant gets stuck in the mud or falls behind, the other members of the herd will help it out. They communicate with each other using low-frequency sounds, some of which are so deep that humans can't hear them.

One of the most amazing things about elephants is their memory. They can remember the locations of waterholes and food sources over vast distances, and they even mourn their dead, showing signs of grief when a member of their herd passes away. In the Serengeti, elephants spend their days grazing on grass and tree bark, and they can eat up to 300 pounds of food in a single day! Despite their massive size, elephants are gentle giants, and seeing them up close is a truly unforgettable experience.

Next on the list is the African buffalo, sometimes called the Cape buffalo. Buffalos are large, powerful animals that can weigh up to 2,000 pounds. They have thick, curved horns that they use to defend themselves from predators. While they might look slow and lumbering, buffalos can be very dangerous when threatened, and they are known for their unpredictable behavior. When they are part of a herd, they feel more confident, but a lone buffalo can be very aggressive if it feels cornered.

Buffalos are herbivores, which means they only eat plants. They spend most of their time grazing on the grasslands of the Serengeti, often in large herds. These herds can be made up of hundreds, even thousands, of buffalo. Like elephants, buffalos are social animals and work together to protect each other from danger. If a predator like a lion tries to attack, the buffalos will form a circle around the weaker members of the herd, using their sharp horns to fend off the attacker. Buffalos might not be as fast or agile as some other animals, but their strength and teamwork make them a force to be reckoned with.

Last but not least, we have the rhinoceros. There are two types of rhinos found in Africa—the black rhino and the white rhino. Both types can be found in the Serengeti, although they are rare and highly endangered. Rhinos are massive creatures, with thick, armor-like skin and a large horn on their nose, which is what makes them so famous.

The black rhino is smaller and more aggressive than the white rhino, but both species are incredibly strong and can charge at speeds of up to 35 miles per hour if they feel threatened.

Rhinos are herbivores, and they spend their days grazing on grasses and leaves. Even though they have poor eyesight, they make up for it with their excellent sense of smell and hearing. Rhinos are solitary animals, preferring to live alone or in small groups. Because of their size and strength, adult rhinos have few natural predators. However, they are in danger because of poaching. Some people illegally hunt rhinos for their horns, which are believed to have special powers in some cultures, even though they are made of the same material as human fingernails. Conservation efforts are underway to protect rhinos from poaching and ensure their survival for future generations.

Together, these five animals—the lion, leopard, elephant, buffalo, and rhinoceros—make up the Big Five of the Serengeti. Seeing any one of these animals in the wild is an incredible experience, but seeing all five is like winning the wildlife jackpot. The Big Five are a symbol of the power, beauty, and diversity of African wildlife, and they play a vital role in the ecosystem of the Serengeti. Each one of them is special in its own way, and they have adapted to survive in one of the most challenging environments on Earth.

For people who visit the Serengeti, the Big Five are often the highlight of their trip. Whether it's watching a pride of lions lounging in the sun, seeing a leopard gracefully leap into a tree, or marveling at the sheer size of an elephant as it moves through the grasslands, these animals leave a lasting impression on everyone who is lucky enough to see them. Conservation efforts are crucial in making sure that the Big Five continue to thrive in the Serengeti. Protecting these animals and their habitat ensures that future generations will have the chance to experience the magic of seeing the Big Five in the wild.

So, the next time you hear someone talk about the Big Five, you'll know that they're talking about some of the most fascinating and powerful animals on the planet. The Big Five aren't just a group of animals—they are symbols of the wild, untamed beauty of Africa, and they remind us of the importance of protecting our planet's incredible wildlife. The Serengeti wouldn't be the same without them, and their presence is a reminder of just how special this part of the world truly is.

Chapter 4: Life in the Grassy Savannas

The grassy savannas of the Serengeti are one of the most fascinating and diverse ecosystems on Earth. These vast, open landscapes stretch as far as the eye can see, covered in golden grasses that sway gently in the breeze. While it may seem like an endless sea of grass, the savannas are teeming with life. From the tiniest insects to the mightiest predators, the Serengeti's grassy plains are home to a wide variety of animals, all perfectly adapted to live in this unique environment. The savanna might look peaceful from a distance, but life here is full of challenges, excitement, and adventure.

One of the first things you notice about the savannas is the wide open space. Unlike dense forests, where trees block your view, the savannas are mostly flat, with just a few scattered trees dotting the horizon. These trees, like the iconic acacia, provide shade and food for many animals. But the heart of the savanna is the grass. This grass is not only the dominant plant but also the foundation of the entire ecosystem. Without the grass, many of the animals in the Serengeti wouldn't be able to survive.

The grass of the savanna is an essential food source for herbivores, or plant-eating animals, which make up a large part of the savanna's population. Animals like zebras, wildebeest, and gazelles spend their days grazing on the nutritious grasses that grow across the plains. These herbivores are constantly on the move, following the rains and the fresh green shoots that sprout up after the rainy season. The animals have to be clever and fast because grazing in the open comes with risks. Predators like lions, cheetahs, and hyenas are always watching, ready to strike at any moment.

Zebras are some of the most common animals in the grassy savannas. With their black-and-white striped coats, they stand out in the golden grass, making it easy to spot them from a distance. But did you know that their stripes actually help them blend in? When zebras stand together in a group, their stripes create a confusing pattern that makes it harder for predators to pick out just one animal to chase. Zebras spend most of their time grazing, using their strong teeth to munch on tough grasses. They live in groups called harems, led by a dominant male, and they are always on the lookout for danger.

Wildebeest, also known as gnus, are another key part of life in the savanna. They might not look as glamorous as zebras with their large, bulky bodies and shaggy beards, but they are one of the most important animals in the Serengeti. Wildebeest are famous for their role in the Great Migration, where millions of them travel in search of fresh grass and water. These animals are strong and resilient, able to travel long distances across the harsh savanna in massive herds. Wildebeest are constantly moving, always looking for the next patch of grass to graze on. Along the way, they face many dangers, from hungry predators to treacherous river crossings.

Gazelles, on the other hand, are much smaller and more delicate-looking than zebras and wildebeest. These graceful animals move lightly across the savanna, using their speed to escape from predators. One of the most well-known species of gazelle in the Serengeti is the Thomson's gazelle, also called a "Tommie." Tommies are incredibly fast and can run up to 50 miles per hour when they need to. They have long, slender legs and large eyes, which help them keep an eye out for predators. Gazelles often graze on the shorter grasses of the savanna, nibbling at the fresh shoots close to the ground.

Of course, life in the grassy savannas isn't just about the herbivores. For every herd of grazing animals, there's a predator lurking nearby, watching and waiting for the right moment to strike. Lions are the most famous predators of the savanna, and they rely on the open plains to spot their prey. Unlike cheetahs, which rely on speed to catch their food, lions use stealth and teamwork. A group of lions, called a pride, will work together to corner and take down large prey like zebras or wildebeest. Once they've made a kill, they feast on the fresh meat, and their full bellies allow them to rest for days before needing to hunt again.

Cheetahs, the fastest land animals in the world, also call the savannas home. These sleek, spotted cats can run at speeds of up to 70 miles per hour, making them perfect hunters for the wide-open spaces of the Serengeti. Cheetahs rely on their incredible speed to chase down gazelles and other small animals. Unlike lions, which hunt in groups, cheetahs hunt alone or in small family groups. After a successful chase, they quickly devour their prey before larger predators like lions or hyenas can steal their meal.

Speaking of hyenas, these scavengers are often misunderstood. While they are famous for their eerie laughter and their habit of stealing food from other animals, hyenas are actually skilled hunters in their own right. In fact, they hunt more often than they scavenge. Hyenas live in clans and work together to bring down prey, sometimes even taking on animals much larger than themselves. Their strong jaws allow them to crush bones and eat almost every part of their kill, which means very little goes to waste.

The savanna is also home to many other animals, each adapted to life in this challenging environment. Giraffes, with their long necks, are perfectly suited for reaching the leaves high up in the trees. They spend their days wandering the savanna, munching on acacia leaves and keeping an eye out for predators. Elephants, the largest land animals, roam the grassy plains in search of food and water. These gentle giants are incredibly important to the savanna ecosystem because they help shape the landscape. When elephants knock down trees to eat the bark or create paths as they move, they open up space for new plants to grow, which in turn provides food for smaller animals.

Birds also play an important role in the savanna. From the brightly colored lilac-breasted roller to the enormous ostrich, the savanna is home to a wide variety of bird species. Some birds, like vultures, are scavengers that help clean up the savanna by eating the remains of animals left behind by predators. Others, like eagles and hawks, are fierce hunters, swooping down from the sky to catch their prey. There are also many smaller birds, like weaver birds, that build intricate nests in the trees and bushes, adding to the diversity of life in the savanna.

Insects are another essential part of life in the savanna, even though they are often overlooked. Termites, for example, play a huge role in the health of the ecosystem. They build massive mounds that can reach several feet high, and these mounds help to aerate the soil, allowing plants to grow. Other insects, like beetles and ants, are busy at work, breaking down plant material and recycling nutrients back into the soil. And, of course, there are the buzzing flies and mosquitoes, which can be annoying to both animals and humans, but they are still an important part of the food chain.

Life in the grassy savannas is all about balance. The herbivores depend on the grass for food, the predators depend on the herbivores for their meals, and the scavengers and insects play their part by cleaning up what's left. The dry and rainy seasons in the Serengeti also play a big role in shaping the lives of the animals that live there. During the rainy season, the grasses grow tall and green, providing plenty of food for the grazing animals. But during the dry season, water becomes scarce, and the animals must travel long distances to find food and water. This constant cycle of growth, survival, and migration keeps the savanna alive and thriving.

The savanna is not just a home for animals. The Maasai people, who have lived in the Serengeti region for centuries, also call the savanna home. The Maasai are semi-nomadic herders, meaning they move with their cattle to find fresh grazing land. Their way of life is deeply connected to the land and the animals of the savanna. They have a deep respect for nature and believe in living in harmony with the environment. The Maasai have learned how to survive in the savanna's harsh conditions, and their vibrant culture adds to the rich diversity of the Serengeti.

In the end, life in the grassy savannas is all about adaptation. Every animal, plant, and even the people who live there have found ways to survive in this ever-changing landscape. It's a place where the strong and the fast thrive, where cooperation is key to survival, and where every living thing plays a role in the delicate balance of nature. The savannas of the Serengeti are a reminder of the beauty and power of the natural world, and they teach us important lessons about how all life is interconnected. Whether it's a lion stalking its prey, a zebra grazing on the grass, or an elephant marching across the plains, life in the grassy savannas is always full of excitement and wonder.

Chapter 5: The Secret World of Lions

Lions are often called the kings and queens of the animal world, but what is it that makes them so special? The Serengeti is one of the best places on Earth to witness these incredible creatures in action. Known for their majestic manes, powerful roars, and social behavior, lions are not just feared predators, but also fascinating animals with complex lives. Behind their fierce reputation lies a secret world of teamwork, family bonds, and survival strategies that help them thrive in the wild. Let's dive into the secret world of lions and explore what life is really like for these iconic big cats.

Lions are unique among the big cats because they are the only ones that live in groups, called prides. A pride of lions can have anywhere from a few to over a dozen members, usually consisting of related females, their cubs, and a few males. Female lions, or lionesses, are the true backbone of the pride. They do most of the hunting and are incredibly skilled at working together to bring down prey. The females are usually sisters, cousins, or mothers and daughters, and they form strong bonds that help the pride stay united and strong.

The male lions in the pride have a different role. They are the protectors, guarding the pride's territory from other lions and predators. Their large manes, which can range in color from golden to black, make them look even more impressive and help them appear bigger and more intimidating to rivals. A male lion's roar can be heard up to five miles away, and it serves as a warning to others to stay out of their territory. While the males don't usually participate in hunting, they are vital to the pride's success by ensuring its safety.

One of the most fascinating aspects of lion life is how they hunt. Despite their powerful build, lions are not the fastest animals in the savanna. They cannot outrun animals like gazelles or zebras over long distances, so they rely on strategy and teamwork to catch their prey. Lionesses are expert hunters, and they work together to stalk and ambush their prey. In the cover of night or early morning, they move quietly through the grass, getting as close as possible without being detected. Then, with a sudden burst of speed, they chase their prey and bring it down with their sharp claws and strong jaws.

The pride works as a team to catch large animals like wildebeest, zebras, and even buffalo. Buffalo, in particular, are very dangerous prey because of their size and strength, so taking one down requires careful planning. The lionesses spread out, some chasing the buffalo from behind while others wait in hiding to cut off its escape. Once the buffalo is tired or cornered, the lions leap onto its back or neck, using their powerful jaws to bring it down. After a successful hunt, the entire pride gathers to share the meal, with the males eating first, followed by the females and cubs.

While lions are often seen as fierce predators, life for them is not always easy. Hunting is difficult, and not every attempt is successful. In fact, lions only succeed in about one out of every four hunts. Sometimes, after a long and exhausting chase, their prey manages to escape. Other times, larger or faster animals like elephants and giraffes are simply too much for the lions to handle. On top of that, lions must compete with other predators, such as hyenas and leopards, who sometimes steal their kills. This means that lions must be smart and adaptable to survive in the wild.

The secret world of lions also involves raising their cubs. Lion cubs are born small, blind, and helpless, and they rely completely on their mothers for food and protection. A lioness usually gives birth to two or three cubs at a time, and she keeps them hidden from the rest of the pride for the first few weeks of their lives. This is because cubs are very vulnerable to danger, and even within their own pride, other lions can be a threat. Male lions, in particular, can be dangerous to cubs that are not their own, as they may see them as competition for the pride's resources.

Once the cubs are strong enough to walk and explore, the mother brings them to meet the rest of the pride. The cubs quickly become part of the pride's daily life, playing with each other, practicing their hunting skills, and learning how to interact with the older lions. Lion cubs are full of energy and spend much of their time chasing each other, pouncing on their mother's tail, or pretending to stalk prey. These playful activities are not just for fun, but also help the cubs develop the skills they will need as adults.

As the cubs grow older, they start to follow the adults on hunts, watching and learning from their mothers and aunts. By the time they are two years old, they are ready to join in on the hunt, though they still have much to learn. Female cubs typically stay with the pride for life, while male cubs eventually leave the pride to start their own or take over a new pride. This process is not easy, and many young male lions face tough challenges when they strike out on their own. They must compete with other males for territory and the chance to join or take over a pride.

One of the most dramatic parts of the lions' secret world is when a new male takes over a pride. Male lions that are strong enough will challenge the existing males for control of the pride. These battles can be fierce and brutal, with both lions using their sharp claws and teeth to fight for dominance. If the challenger wins, he takes over the pride and becomes its new leader. Unfortunately, this often means that any cubs fathered by the previous male are in danger, as the new male may kill them to make sure only his offspring survive.

Lions are not just fierce predators and protective parents, though. They also have a softer side that shows how close their family bonds really are. Lions spend a lot of time grooming each other, licking and nuzzling to strengthen their relationships. This grooming helps to keep their fur clean and free from parasites, but it also shows affection and reinforces the pride's social bonds. Lions often rest together in large groups, with cubs snuggled up next to their mothers and other lions lying in close contact. These social behaviors show just how important family is to lions, and they help the pride stay united and strong.

Lions are also very vocal animals. While their roar is the most famous sound they make, lions communicate with each other in many different ways. They use growls, grunts, and purrs to express different emotions, from warning off intruders to showing affection to each other. When a pride of lions is together, you can often hear them communicating with soft chuffing sounds, which are a friendly way of saying hello. Lions also use body language to communicate, such as nuzzling or rubbing their heads together to show trust and affection.

Lions face many challenges in the wild, from finding enough food to dealing with rival predators. But one of the biggest threats to lions today comes from humans. As human populations grow and expand into lion territory, lions are losing their natural habitat. In some areas, lions come into conflict with farmers when they prey on livestock, leading to tensions between people and lions. Conservation efforts are now in place to protect lions and their habitat, and many organizations are working hard to ensure that future generations can continue to witness the beauty and majesty of lions in the wild.

Despite these challenges, lions remain one of the most powerful and awe-inspiring animals on Earth. They are more than just kings and queens of the savanna—they are symbols of strength, teamwork, and survival. Their complex social structures, incredible hunting abilities, and deep family bonds make them truly unique creatures. By understanding the secret world of lions, we can gain a greater appreciation for these magnificent animals and the important role they play in the Serengeti's ecosystem. Whether they are roaring in the distance, chasing down prey, or resting with their cubs, lions continue to captivate and inspire us with their beauty, power, and grace.

Chapter 6: How Elephants Rule the Serengeti

Elephants are the true giants of the Serengeti, not just because of their size but because of the incredible impact they have on the environment. These gentle giants are among the most fascinating animals in the world, and they play a unique role in shaping the landscape of the Serengeti and maintaining the delicate balance of its ecosystem. Their presence is vital for other animals and plants, and their behavior is both impressive and important to the survival of many species. In a way, elephants really do rule the Serengeti, but not through fear or force—through their sheer size, intelligence, and actions that benefit the entire savanna.

When you think of elephants, the first thing that comes to mind is likely their enormous size. Adult African elephants can weigh up to 12,000 pounds and stand as tall as 13 feet at the shoulder. Their large ears, long trunks, and massive tusks make them unmistakable. But being big isn't the only thing that makes elephants rulers of the Serengeti. What really sets them apart is how they use their size and strength to shape their environment. Elephants are known as "ecosystem engineers," which means they change the landscape in ways that create habitats for other species. For example, when elephants knock down trees to get to the leaves or bark, they open up the grasslands, allowing smaller plants to grow and providing food for other animals like zebras, antelopes, and gazelles.

Elephants are also constantly on the move. They roam across vast distances in search of food and water, and as they travel, they leave a trail of broken branches, trampled plants, and disturbed soil. While this might sound destructive, it actually helps the Serengeti stay healthy. By knocking down old trees and bushes, elephants make space for new plants to grow, and their heavy feet churn up the soil, helping seeds take root. In this way, elephants help keep the grasslands from becoming overgrown with trees and bushes, which allows more sunlight to reach the ground and encourages a wider variety of plants to grow. This benefits the entire ecosystem, from the smallest insects to the largest predators.

One of the most remarkable things about elephants is their trunks. An elephant's trunk is a combination of its nose and upper lip, and it is incredibly versatile. Elephants use their trunks to do everything from picking up tiny objects, like a single blade of grass, to pulling down entire tree branches. They use their trunks to drink by sucking up water and then squirting it into their mouths, and they also use them to shower themselves, spraying water or dust over their bodies to cool down or protect their skin from the sun. Elephants' trunks are also powerful tools for communication. They can make deep rumbling sounds that travel for miles, allowing elephants to communicate with each other over long distances. These sounds are so low-pitched that humans can't even hear them, but other elephants can.

Elephants are known for their intelligence, and they have some of the largest brains of any land animal. They are capable of solving problems, using tools, and showing emotions like empathy and grief. In fact, elephants are one of the few animals that seem to mourn their dead. When an elephant in the herd dies, the others will gather around the body, touching it with their trunks and standing quietly, almost as if they are paying their respects. Elephants have even been seen returning to the bones of dead elephants years later, gently touching the bones as if they remember the individual who once lived. This strong emotional connection shows just how deep the bonds between elephants can be.

Elephants live in herds, and these herds are usually led by the oldest female, called the matriarch. The matriarch is the most experienced and knowledgeable member of the herd, and she is responsible for leading the group to food and water, as well as teaching the younger elephants how to survive. The matriarch plays a crucial role during tough times, such as during droughts when food and water are scarce. Her memory of where to find waterholes and food sources during past droughts can mean the difference between life and death for the herd. Elephants have incredible memories, and the matriarch uses this skill to guide her family through the challenges of life in the Serengeti.

In addition to their intelligence, elephants are highly social animals. They form close bonds with each other, and family is at the heart of elephant society. The herd usually consists of related females and their calves, while males leave the herd when they reach adolescence and live on their own or in small groups with other males. The females in the herd work together to raise and protect their young. Elephant calves are vulnerable when they are born, and they rely on their mothers and aunts to take care of them. The entire herd helps raise the calves, teaching them how to find food and water, how to use their trunks, and how to interact with other elephants. The bond between a mother and her calf is especially strong, and the calf will stay close to its mother for several years, learning everything it needs to know to survive in the wild.

Elephants communicate with each other in many ways, using a combination of sounds, body language, and touch. In addition to the deep rumbling sounds they make with their trunks, elephants also use their large ears to signal their mood. If an elephant feels threatened or angry, it will flap its ears and raise its trunk to make itself look bigger and more intimidating. On the other hand, elephants will gently touch each other with their trunks to show affection or comfort. Elephants are also known to wrap their trunks around each other in a gesture that seems similar to a hug.

Water is incredibly important to elephants, and they spend a lot of time searching for it. During the dry season, when water sources are scarce, elephants will dig into dry riverbeds with their trunks and tusks to find underground water. These waterholes often become lifesaving resources for other animals, too. Zebras, antelopes, and even predators like lions will come to drink from the waterholes that elephants create. In this way, elephants help support the survival of many other species in the Serengeti. When elephants find water, they don't just drink it—they also love to splash and play in it. Watching a herd of elephants bathing in a river or watering hole is a joyful sight. They spray water over their bodies, roll around in the mud, and sometimes even dunk each other under the water. This playful behavior not only cools them down but also helps protect their skin from the sun and insects.

Elephants are known for their peaceful nature, but they can be dangerous when they feel threatened or when their calves are in danger. Despite their size, elephants are surprisingly fast and can charge at speeds of up to 25 miles per hour. When an elephant charges, it can be a terrifying sight, with its ears flared out, trunk raised, and tusks pointed forward. This behavior is usually a warning to potential threats to stay away. Elephants are protective of their families, and they will do whatever it takes to keep their calves safe from predators like lions and hyenas. In fact, predators rarely attack healthy adult elephants because of their size and strength, but they do sometimes target young calves. When this happens, the entire herd comes together to form a protective circle around the calves, using their bodies and tusks to fend off any attackers.

Elephants also have a powerful influence on the Serengeti's water systems. In addition to creating waterholes, they also help keep rivers and lakes clear by knocking over trees and shrubs that block the flow of water. Without elephants, many of the Serengeti's water sources would become clogged with vegetation, making it harder for animals to access clean drinking water. By keeping these water systems healthy, elephants help ensure that the entire ecosystem has the resources it needs to thrive.

While elephants are magnificent rulers of the Serengeti, they face serious challenges today. One of the biggest threats to elephants is poaching. Elephants are hunted for their tusks, which are made of valuable ivory. Poachers kill elephants to sell their ivory on the black market, and this illegal trade has devastated elephant populations in many parts of Africa. Conservation efforts are now in place to protect elephants and reduce poaching, but the fight to save these incredible animals is far from over. Elephants are also losing their habitat as human populations expand and more land is used for farming and development. This habitat loss makes it harder for elephants to find food and water, and it also increases the chances of conflict between elephants and humans.

Despite these challenges, elephants remain one of the most awe-inspiring animals on Earth. They are gentle giants with incredible intelligence, strong family bonds, and a deep connection to the land they call home. Their role as ecosystem engineers makes them vital to the health of the Serengeti, and their presence supports the survival of countless other species. Whether they are creating waterholes, knocking down trees, or leading their herds across the savanna, elephants truly do rule the Serengeti in a way that no other animal can. Their power comes not from aggression or dominance, but from their ability to shape the world around them and support the entire ecosystem in which they live. By understanding the secret world of elephants, we can appreciate the important role they play in keeping the Serengeti alive and thriving.

Chapter 7: Zebras and Wildebeest on the Move

In the Serengeti, two animals that are often seen traveling together in great numbers are zebras and wildebeest. These two species have a unique relationship and are among the most iconic animals of the African plains. Both zebras and wildebeest are constantly on the move, always in search of food and water as the seasons change across the vast landscape. Their incredible journeys are a big part of what makes the Serengeti so special. Every year, zebras and wildebeest take part in one of the most astonishing natural events on Earth: the Great Migration, where millions of these animals trek across the Serengeti in a search for greener pastures. But their lives are about much more than just the migration; their daily movements and behaviors help define the rhythms of life on the savanna.

Zebras and wildebeest are both herbivores, which means they eat plants. Their favorite meals are grasses that cover the Serengeti plains. The grasses in this region are rich and nutritious, but they can be hard to find during certain times of the year, especially when the dry season arrives, and water becomes scarce. When the rains stop and the grass dries up, these animals have to move, and this is when their epic journeys begin. Zebras and wildebeest have to be constantly on the lookout for new areas with fresh grass to eat and water to drink, so they are always moving across the savanna, following the seasonal rains that bring life to the land.

What's interesting about zebras and wildebeest is that even though they are different species, they often travel together. You might wonder why that is. It turns out that zebras and wildebeest have a lot to gain from sticking together. While zebras are more alert and have excellent eyesight and hearing, wildebeest have a better sense of direction and can remember where the best grazing lands are located. By traveling together, zebras and wildebeest benefit from each other's strengths. Zebras act as lookouts, keeping an eye out for danger, while wildebeest can lead the way to fresh grass and water. This teamwork helps them both survive the challenges of life in the Serengeti.

Zebras are known for their striking black and white stripes, and no two zebras have the same stripe pattern. Each zebra's stripes are unique, almost like a fingerprint. These stripes serve many purposes. For one, they help camouflage the zebras in the tall grasses of the savanna, confusing predators like lions and hyenas. When zebras are grouped together, their stripes can make it difficult for predators to single out one animal to attack. The stripes also help zebras stay cool in the hot African sun. Scientists believe that the different colors of the stripes create air currents around the zebra's body, which helps cool them down. Another amazing thing about zebra stripes is that they help zebras recognize each other. In a large herd of zebras, each individual can identify other members of the herd by their unique stripe patterns.

Wildebeest, on the other hand, are large, sturdy animals with long faces and curved horns. They have shaggy manes and tails, and their fur is a mix of gray, brown, and black. While wildebeest may not be as flashy as zebras, they are incredible runners and can cover great distances when they need to escape from danger. Wildebeest are known for their endurance, and during the Great Migration, they travel hundreds of miles in search of food and water. Their ability to keep moving, even in the face of extreme conditions, is one of the reasons why they are such successful survivors in the Serengeti.

The Great Migration is one of the most famous events in the animal kingdom, and it's an essential part of life for zebras and wildebeest. Every year, around two million wildebeest, along with hundreds of thousands of zebras, make the journey from the southern Serengeti to the northern areas and into Kenya's Masai Mara. The migration follows the seasonal rains, with the animals moving in a giant circular path across the plains in search of fresh grazing lands. The migration is not just a journey for food and water; it's also a journey of survival. Along the way, these animals face many dangers, including predators like lions, cheetahs, and crocodiles, who wait for the herds at river crossings, hoping to catch a meal. Despite these dangers, the zebras and wildebeest continue their journey year after year, driven by an instinct to survive and find the resources they need.

One of the most dramatic moments of the Great Migration is the crossing of the Mara River. This river is full of powerful currents, and its waters are home to crocodiles that lie in wait for the migrating animals. When the zebras and wildebeest reach the river, they gather in large numbers along the banks, hesitating for a moment before plunging into the water. The crossing is chaotic and dangerous, with some animals making it to the other side while others fall victim to the fast-moving water or the waiting crocodiles. But crossing the river is necessary for the herds to reach the lush grasslands on the other side, and so they take the risk. Watching the river crossing is one of the most thrilling wildlife spectacles in the world, showcasing the determination and resilience of these animals.

Life for zebras and wildebeest is not just about the Great Migration, though. Even when they are not on the move, they are constantly grazing and looking for food. Zebras and wildebeest have different grazing habits that allow them to share the same land without competing too much for food. Zebras prefer to eat the taller grasses, while wildebeest focus on the shorter, fresher grasses. This division of labor means that they can graze together without exhausting the food supply too quickly. In this way, zebras and wildebeest help maintain the balance of the Serengeti's grasslands, ensuring that the ecosystem remains healthy for all the animals that live there.

Another important aspect of zebra and wildebeest life is their social structure. Zebras live in small family groups called harems, which consist of one male, several females, and their offspring. The male, called a stallion, is very protective of his group and will fight off other males to keep his harem together. Wildebeest, on the other hand, live in larger herds that can number in the thousands. These herds are constantly changing, with individuals joining and leaving as they move across the plains. Living in large groups helps protect both zebras and wildebeest from predators. There is safety in numbers, and by sticking together, these animals can watch out for each other and reduce the chances of being attacked.

Zebras and wildebeest are also important prey animals in the Serengeti. Predators like lions, cheetahs, and hyenas rely on these herbivores for food. However, zebras and wildebeest have developed ways to defend themselves. Zebras are known to kick with incredible force, and a well-placed kick from a zebra's powerful hind legs can seriously injure a predator. Wildebeest, with their large horns, will form a defensive circle around their young, standing shoulder to shoulder to protect the calves from danger. While predators are always a threat, zebras and wildebeest are not easy targets, and many escape attacks by using their speed and strength.

Despite the challenges they face, zebras and wildebeest thrive in the Serengeti. Their ability to travel long distances, their cooperation with each other, and their defensive strategies all contribute to their survival in this harsh environment. The relationship between zebras and wildebeest is a perfect example of how animals can work together to survive, even in the face of difficult conditions. By sticking together and relying on each other's strengths, zebras and wildebeest have adapted to life on the move, and their incredible migrations are a testament to their resilience and determination.

The Serengeti would not be the same without these two iconic species. Zebras, with their distinctive stripes and social behavior, and wildebeest, with their endurance and vast herds, are a crucial part of the ecosystem. Their movements across the plains help shape the landscape, ensuring that the grasslands remain healthy and diverse. Their migration is one of the greatest natural wonders of the world, a spectacle of survival, teamwork, and the never-ending search for the resources they need to thrive. Watching zebras and wildebeest on the move is like witnessing the heartbeat of the Serengeti, as these animals follow the rhythms of nature and remind us of the incredible power and beauty of life in the wild.

Chapter 8: Cheetahs: Speeding Through the Plains

In the Serengeti, there is one animal that stands out for its incredible speed and agility: the cheetah. Known as the fastest land animal on Earth, cheetahs are like the sports cars of the animal kingdom, speeding through the open plains in pursuit of their prey. These sleek, spotted cats are not only built for speed but are also masters of stealth and precision, making them some of the most efficient hunters in the wild. Life for a cheetah is all about the chase, and their ability to run faster than any other animal is key to their survival. But there's much more to cheetahs than just their speed; they have fascinating behaviors, unique physical traits, and face many challenges in the Serengeti's vast grasslands.

Cheetahs are instantly recognizable thanks to their distinctive black spots, which cover their golden-yellow fur. These spots act as camouflage, helping them blend into the tall grasses of the savanna. Unlike other big cats, cheetahs don't rely on strength or size to catch their prey. Instead, they depend on their incredible speed and acceleration, which allow them to outrun almost any animal. A cheetah can go from a standstill to running at speeds of up to 60 to 70 miles per hour in just a few seconds! That's faster than most cars on a highway. But cheetahs aren't just fast sprinters; they are also incredibly nimble, able to change direction quickly while running at high speeds, which helps them stay close to their prey even when it tries to escape by zigzagging.

What makes cheetahs so fast? It's all about their special physical adaptations. Cheetahs have long, slim bodies and lightweight frames, which make them perfectly designed for running. Their legs are long and muscular, and their spine is extremely flexible, allowing them to stretch their bodies out fully when they run. This gives them an extra-long stride, so they cover more ground with each step. Cheetahs also have large nasal passages and lungs, which allow them to take in more oxygen while running. Their hearts and lungs are much larger than those of other animals of the same size, giving them the stamina they need for their lightning-fast sprints. Additionally, cheetahs have special pads on their paws that give them extra grip, similar to the tread on a car tire, helping them maintain traction as they speed across the ground.

Despite their amazing speed, cheetahs can only maintain their top speed for short bursts. A full-speed chase lasts less than a minute because sprinting at such high speeds uses up a lot of energy and overheats their bodies. After a chase, a cheetah must rest for a while to recover. This means that if they don't catch their prey quickly, they often have to give up the chase and wait for another opportunity. Cheetahs usually hunt during the day, unlike many other predators in the Serengeti, which are more active at night. This daytime hunting gives cheetahs an advantage because there is less competition from other big cats like lions and leopards, but it also means they have to deal with the intense heat of the African sun.

Cheetahs are expert hunters, and their hunting technique is all about speed and surprise. Cheetahs rely on their excellent eyesight to spot their prey from a distance. Once they've chosen a target, they use their stealth to get as close as possible before launching their high-speed chase. Cheetahs typically hunt smaller, fast-moving animals like gazelles, impalas, and young wildebeests. They prefer these animals because they are light enough for the cheetah to overpower and catch without too much difficulty. When the time is right, the cheetah bursts into action, sprinting after its prey with incredible speed. As they close in, cheetahs use their long tails to help them balance as they make quick turns to follow their prey's movements. Finally, with a swift swipe of their front paws or a powerful bite to the throat, the cheetah brings down its target.

Although cheetahs are expert hunters, their lives aren't easy. One of the biggest challenges cheetahs face is that they often have to compete with other predators for their hard-earned meals. Even though cheetahs are fast and efficient hunters, they are not the strongest animals in the Serengeti. After catching their prey, cheetahs sometimes have their food stolen by larger predators like lions, hyenas, and leopards. These animals are stronger and more aggressive, and they will chase cheetahs away from their kills. This means that even after the effort of a high-speed chase, a cheetah might lose its meal to another predator. Because of this, cheetahs usually try to eat their prey quickly after a successful hunt to avoid attracting attention from other animals. In fact, they often drag their catch to a hidden spot where they can eat in peace.

Cheetahs also have unique social behaviors. Unlike lions, which live in large prides, cheetahs are more solitary animals. Adult female cheetahs live on their own, except when they are raising cubs. They have large home ranges, or territories, that they roam in search of food. Male cheetahs, however, are a bit different. While some male cheetahs live alone, others form small groups called coalitions, usually made up of brothers from the same litter. These coalitions stick together throughout their lives, hunting and patrolling their territory as a team. By working together, male cheetahs can defend their territory more effectively and increase their chances of finding food.

Raising cheetah cubs is no easy task for a mother cheetah. After a pregnancy of about three months, a female cheetah gives birth to a litter of cubs, usually between two and six. Cheetah cubs are born blind and helpless, relying entirely on their mother for protection and care. For the first few weeks of their lives, the cubs stay hidden in a den, where the mother keeps them safe from predators. As the cubs grow older, the mother moves them from place to place to avoid detection by lions, hyenas, or other threats. Cheetah cubs have a special coat of fur when they are young, with a mane of long, silver-gray hair on their backs. This mane helps them blend into the tall grass and may also make them look larger than they really are, deterring potential predators.

As they grow, cheetah cubs begin to learn how to hunt by watching their mother. Around six months of age, they start practicing hunting techniques, chasing each other and small animals in playful mock-hunts. The mother cheetah is very patient during this time, teaching her cubs the skills they will need to survive on their own. By the time they are about a year and a half old, cheetah cubs are ready to leave their mother and start life on their own, although siblings often stay together for a while before eventually going their separate ways.

Life for cheetahs in the Serengeti can be tough, and their population has faced many challenges over the years. Habitat loss, human-wildlife conflict, and competition with other predators have all contributed to the decline of cheetah numbers in the wild. Because cheetahs need large, open spaces to hunt and live, they are particularly vulnerable to changes in the environment. In many areas, human settlements have expanded into the cheetahs' natural habitat, making it harder for them to find food and safe places to live. Conservation efforts are underway to protect cheetah populations and ensure that these magnificent animals continue to thrive in the wild. Organizations are working to create protected areas where cheetahs can hunt and live without the threat of human interference. There are also efforts to educate people living near cheetah habitats about how to coexist peacefully with these animals, helping to reduce conflicts between humans and wildlife.

Another challenge cheetahs face is their relatively low genetic diversity. Because there are so few cheetahs left in the wild, the gene pool is smaller, which can make it harder for them to adapt to changing environments or recover from disease outbreaks. Scientists are studying cheetahs to better understand their genetic makeup and find ways to help protect them from the risks associated with low genetic diversity.

By learning more about cheetahs and their needs, conservationists hope to ensure that future generations of cheetahs can continue to speed across the plains of the Serengeti.

Cheetahs are truly remarkable animals, and their role in the Serengeti ecosystem is vital. As skilled hunters, they help keep the populations of herbivores like gazelles in balance, ensuring that the grasslands remain healthy and diverse. Their speed and agility make them one of the most exciting animals to watch in the wild, and seeing a cheetah in full sprint is a sight that leaves a lasting impression. Cheetahs remind us of the beauty and power of nature and the importance of protecting the incredible wildlife that calls the Serengeti home. As long as conservation efforts continue, there is hope that these speedy cats will continue to race across the savanna for generations to come, thrilling anyone lucky enough to witness their incredible talents in action.

Chapter 9: Giraffes: Tall Guardians of the Serengeti

Giraffes are like the gentle giants of the Serengeti, towering over the grasslands with their long necks and graceful presence. As the tallest land animals in the world, they stand out in the vast plains, easily spotted from far away as they stroll through the savannas. With their legs as long as some humans are tall and their necks stretching high into the sky, giraffes are truly unique creatures. But these "tall guardians" of the Serengeti do much more than just stand out because of their height. They play a vital role in keeping the ecosystem healthy, and their behavior, diet, and way of life are fascinating to explore.

Giraffes can grow to be as tall as 18 feet, with males typically being taller than females. Their long necks help them reach food that other animals can't, making them the Serengeti's natural tree-trimmers. While most of the animals that live on the plains graze on grass, giraffes prefer to browse on leaves, particularly from acacia trees. Acacia trees are known for their thorny branches, but that doesn't stop giraffes from enjoying their leaves. Giraffes use their long, purple tongues—up to 18 inches long—to skillfully pluck leaves from between the thorns. Their tongues are tough and leathery, which protects them from getting pricked. This feeding habit allows giraffes to access a food source that few other animals can, and by munching on the tops of trees, giraffes help prune them, which encourages new growth and keeps the vegetation of the Serengeti in balance.

While their necks are certainly long, giraffes only have seven neck vertebrae, just like humans. However, each of these bones is much larger, and they are connected by flexible joints that allow giraffes to stretch and bend their necks to reach leaves high in the treetops. This amazing adaptation is perfect for life in the savanna, where tall trees are common, and being able to reach the freshest leaves gives giraffes a significant advantage. They can eat up to 75 pounds of leaves a day, and their height means they don't have to compete with many other animals for food. But giraffes aren't just eating machines—they're also an important part of the ecosystem. As they move from tree to tree, giraffes help spread seeds across the savanna. This helps new plants grow, supporting the overall health of the environment.

Giraffes' height gives them another advantage in the Serengeti—they act as the watchtowers of the savanna. Their long necks allow them to see far across the plains, which helps them keep an eye out for predators like lions and hyenas. When a giraffe senses danger, it stands still and watches closely, its head raised high above the grass. Other animals in the area, like zebras and antelopes, will often pay attention to what the giraffes are doing. If the giraffes seem relaxed, the other animals know it's safe to continue grazing. But if a giraffe suddenly becomes alert and starts to move away, it's often a sign that a predator is nearby. In this way, giraffes act like silent sentinels, helping to warn other animals of potential threats.

Although giraffes are generally peaceful and calm animals, they are not defenseless. They have incredibly powerful legs, and a well-placed kick from a giraffe can be deadly to a predator like a lion. Giraffes use their strong legs to defend themselves, especially when they are protecting their young. Baby giraffes, called calves, are vulnerable to attacks from predators, so mother giraffes are always on high alert. A giraffe calf is born after about 15 months of pregnancy, and when it's born, it can stand and walk within hours. Even though giraffe calves are around six feet tall when they're born, they are still small compared to adult giraffes and are at risk of being hunted by lions or hyenas. But with their mothers nearby to protect them, giraffe calves have a good chance of growing up safely.

Life for giraffes is not just about eating leaves and avoiding predators; they also have interesting social structures. Giraffes live in loose groups called towers, and these groups can change from day to day. A tower might consist of just a few individuals or as many as 30 giraffes, and the makeup of the group often shifts as giraffes come and go. Unlike some animals that have strong hierarchies or close-knit family groups, giraffes are more independent, and their social bonds are more relaxed. Males, called bulls, are especially solitary. They often wander alone or in small bachelor groups, only coming together with females during mating season.

Male giraffes also engage in a behavior known as "necking," where they use their necks to spar with each other in a show of strength. During these battles, bulls swing their heads at each other, striking their opponent's body or neck with their bony skulls. While this might sound dangerous, most necking contests don't result in serious injuries. Instead, it's a way for male giraffes to establish dominance and show off their strength. The giraffe that wins the contest often gets the attention of nearby females and has a better chance of mating.

Despite their impressive size and strength, giraffes face many challenges in the wild. One of the biggest threats to giraffes in the Serengeti is habitat loss. As human populations grow, more land is being used for farming and settlements, which reduces the natural habitat available for giraffes to live and feed. In some areas, giraffes have to compete with livestock for food and water, which can put additional strain on their survival. Another threat to giraffes is illegal poaching. While giraffes are not hunted as often as some other animals like elephants or rhinos, they are still sometimes targeted for their meat or hides. Conservation efforts are underway to protect giraffe populations, but their numbers have declined in many areas over the past few decades.

In recent years, giraffes have been classified as vulnerable, meaning they are at risk of becoming endangered if action is not taken to protect them. Conservation organizations are working to raise awareness about the threats facing giraffes and are working with local communities to protect giraffe habitats. One important aspect of giraffe conservation is the creation of protected areas where giraffes can live without the pressure of human development. In the Serengeti, these protected areas help ensure that giraffes have the space they need to roam and find food. Conservationists are also studying giraffe populations to better understand their behavior, social structures, and migration patterns, which can help in developing strategies to protect them in the future.

Another key aspect of giraffe conservation is educating people about the importance of preserving these magnificent animals. Giraffes are an iconic part of the African landscape, and they play a crucial role in maintaining the balance of the ecosystem. By raising awareness about the challenges giraffes face, conservationists hope to inspire people to take action to protect them. This might involve supporting anti-poaching efforts, reducing habitat destruction, or promoting ecotourism, where visitors to the Serengeti can learn about giraffes and other wildlife while contributing to conservation efforts.

Giraffes are not just important for the environment—they also hold a special place in the hearts of people around the world. Their gentle nature, long necks, and spotted coats make them one of the most beloved animals in the Serengeti. For visitors to the Serengeti, seeing a giraffe in the wild is an unforgettable experience. Whether they are watching a giraffe gracefully walk across the plains or observing a mother giraffe feeding her calf, people are often amazed by these incredible animals. Giraffes remind us of the beauty and diversity of life on Earth, and they serve as a symbol of the need to protect and preserve the natural world.

In the Serengeti, giraffes are more than just tall animals—they are an essential part of the ecosystem, helping to shape the landscape and maintain the balance of nature. Their long necks give them access to food that other animals can't reach, and their gentle presence serves as a watchful guardian over the savanna. As they move gracefully through the grasslands, giraffes help spread seeds, prune trees, and keep an eye out for danger. They are peaceful yet powerful, and their unique adaptations make them one of the most fascinating creatures in the Serengeti. By learning more about giraffes and the challenges they face, we can all play a part in ensuring that these tall guardians continue to thrive in the wild for generations to come.

Chapter 10: Birds of the Serengeti Sky

The Serengeti is a magical place, filled with a wide variety of animals roaming across its vast plains. While many people may first think of lions, elephants, and giraffes when imagining the Serengeti, there's another group of incredible creatures that soar high above the ground, filling the skies with life and beauty—birds. The birds of the Serengeti are as diverse and remarkable as the land they call home. From the smallest of songbirds to the largest of raptors, these feathered creatures play an important role in the ecosystem, each with their own special characteristics and behaviors.

When you look up at the Serengeti sky, you might first notice the magnificent vultures circling above. Vultures are often misunderstood, but they are some of the most important birds in the Serengeti. As scavengers, vultures help clean up the environment by feeding on the remains of animals that have died. Without vultures, the Serengeti would be a much messier place, with carcasses left to rot and potentially spread disease. There are several types of vultures in the Serengeti, including the white-backed vulture and the Rüppell's vulture. These large birds have incredible eyesight and can spot a meal from miles away. Once they find a dead animal, they swoop down to feed, using their strong beaks to tear through tough skin and meat. While their dining habits may seem gross to us, vultures play a critical role in keeping the Serengeti healthy and free from decaying animals.

But vultures aren't the only birds that capture attention in the Serengeti skies. Another impressive bird of prey is the martial eagle. This powerful raptor is one of the largest eagles in Africa, with a wingspan that can reach up to 8 feet! Martial eagles are skilled hunters, capable of taking down prey as large as small antelopes. They use their sharp talons and strong beaks to catch and eat animals like hares, birds, and even reptiles. Their keen eyesight allows them to spot their prey from high up in the air, and once they see their target, they dive down at incredible speeds to snatch it up. Martial eagles are known for their strength and fierce hunting skills, making them the top predators of the bird world in the Serengeti.

While birds of prey like vultures and eagles are often admired for their size and power, the Serengeti is also home to many smaller, yet equally fascinating, bird species. Take the lilac-breasted roller, for example. This brightly colored bird is a favorite among birdwatchers because of its stunning plumage. Its feathers are a vibrant mix of blues, greens, and purples, making it one of the most eye-catching birds in the Serengeti. The lilac-breasted roller gets its name from its rolling flight pattern, which it performs during mating displays or to ward off rivals. Although it may not be as large as an eagle or as strong as a vulture, this beautiful bird brings color and joy to the Serengeti with its graceful flight and striking appearance.

Another fascinating bird you might encounter in the Serengeti is the ostrich. Ostriches are the largest birds on Earth, but unlike many other birds, they cannot fly. Instead, ostriches are built for running. With their long legs and powerful muscles, ostriches can sprint up to 45 miles per hour, making them the fastest land birds in the world. Ostriches use their incredible speed to escape predators like lions or hyenas. They can also kick with their strong legs, delivering a powerful blow if they need to defend themselves. Even though they can't fly, ostriches are still perfectly adapted to life in the Serengeti, where they roam the grasslands in search of food like seeds, insects, and plants. Their long necks allow them to spot danger from a distance, and their speed helps them outrun many of their predators.

If you're lucky, you might also spot a secretary bird striding across the savanna. This unusual-looking bird has long legs, a sharp beak, and a striking crest of feathers on its head that makes it look a bit like a bird in fancy dress. Unlike most birds of prey that soar through the skies, secretary birds prefer to hunt on foot. They walk across the grasslands, using their strong legs to stomp on their prey, which includes snakes, lizards, and small mammals. Secretary birds are especially famous for their ability to hunt and kill venomous snakes. With their quick reflexes and powerful kicks, they can dispatch a snake before it has a chance to strike. Secretary birds are a rare sight, but their unique hunting style and elegant appearance make them one of the most interesting birds in the Serengeti.

While some birds in the Serengeti are known for their hunting abilities, others are celebrated for their songs. The serenade of the white-bellied go-away bird is a common sound in the Serengeti. These birds get their name from the loud "go-away" call they make, which some people think sounds like they are telling others to stay away! Despite their strange name, these birds are social creatures that live in small groups and are often seen hopping through trees in search of fruit and leaves to eat. Their soft gray feathers and white bellies may not be as colorful as some other birds, but their distinctive call ensures that they are never overlooked.

Another group of birds that are easy to spot in the Serengeti are the flamingos, particularly around the lakes and wetlands. These long-legged, pink-feathered birds are famous for their graceful beauty and the way they stand on one leg while feeding. Flamingos get their pink color from the food they eat—tiny shrimp and algae that contain special pigments. As they filter these foods through their beaks, they slowly turn pink, a color that only grows more vibrant as they age. Flamingos live in large colonies, sometimes gathering in groups of thousands, creating an incredible sight when they take to the air in unison, forming a sea of pink wings against the blue sky.

The crowned crane is another bird that adds beauty to the Serengeti. With its golden, spiky crown of feathers and long, slender neck, the crowned crane is one of the most striking birds in Africa. These elegant birds are known for their elaborate courtship dances, where they leap into the air, bow, and spread their wings in graceful displays. Crowned cranes live in wetlands and grasslands, where they feed on insects, seeds, and small animals. Their large, loud calls can be heard across the plains, adding to the symphony of bird sounds that fill the Serengeti.

In addition to these standout species, the Serengeti is home to many other types of birds, each playing a unique role in the ecosystem. Weaver birds, for example, are small, energetic birds known for their incredible nest-building skills. Using grass and other plant materials, weaver birds create intricate, woven nests that hang from tree branches. These nests are not only sturdy and safe but are also beautifully crafted, showcasing the birds' impressive construction abilities. Weaver birds are also very social, often living in large colonies where hundreds of nests can be found in a single tree.

Then, there are the hornbills, with their distinctive curved bills. These birds have a quirky and fascinating behavior when it comes to nesting. When a female hornbill is ready to lay her eggs, she and her mate will find a tree hole. The female will then seal herself inside the hole using mud and food brought by her mate, leaving only a small slit through which the male can pass her food. She stays in the hole until the chicks are ready to leave the nest, safe from predators during this vulnerable time.

From the ground-dwelling ostrich to the high-flying vultures, birds in the Serengeti are as varied as they are numerous. Each species has adapted in its own way to survive in this unique environment. Whether they're soaring through the skies in search of prey, building intricate nests in the trees, or singing sweet songs from the branches, the birds of the Serengeti are an essential part of what makes this region so special. They help maintain the balance of nature, clean up the environment, and bring beauty and life to the skies.

As you explore the Serengeti, you'll come to realize that it's not just the big animals on the ground that make this place so incredible—it's the birds above, too. From the largest eagle to the tiniest songbird, the Serengeti's birdlife is full of surprises, each species with its own unique role in the ecosystem. These birds remind us that the Serengeti is a place of endless wonder, where every creature, no matter how big or small, has an important part to play. Watching birds soar across the sky, hearing their calls fill the air, and seeing their graceful movements are all part of the magic of the Serengeti. They are the guardians of the skies, the singers of the plains, and the unseen helpers that keep this remarkable ecosystem in balance.

Chapter 11: The Hidden Lives of Hyenas

Hyenas are some of the most misunderstood animals in the Serengeti. They are often portrayed as sneaky scavengers in stories and movies, but there's so much more to them than meets the eye. In reality, hyenas are incredibly complex animals with unique behaviors, social structures, and survival skills that make them fascinating creatures. If you look beyond the myths and misconceptions, you'll discover that the hidden lives of hyenas are filled with teamwork, intelligence, and some surprising habits.

First, let's talk about what kind of animal a hyena really is. Hyenas are not part of the dog family, even though they might look similar. They actually belong to their own special family called Hyaenidae. In the Serengeti, the most common type of hyena is the spotted hyena, which is the largest of the four species of hyenas in the world. Spotted hyenas have light brown or grayish fur covered in dark spots, and they can weigh up to 140 pounds. They have strong, muscular bodies, especially in their front legs, which gives them a sloping back. Their powerful jaws and teeth allow them to crush through bones, which is something most other predators can't do.

One of the most interesting things about hyenas is how social they are. Spotted hyenas live in groups called clans, which can have anywhere from a few individuals to over 80 members. A clan of hyenas is ruled by a dominant female, making them one of the few matriarchal societies in the animal kingdom. The females are larger and stronger than the males, and they hold all the power within the group. The top-ranking female, called the matriarch, is in charge, and her daughters usually inherit her high rank. Male hyenas, on the other hand, rank lower and often leave the clan when they reach adulthood to find another clan to join.

Within a hyena clan, each member has a specific rank in the social hierarchy. Hyenas communicate their rank and status through various behaviors, including vocalizations, body language, and even scent marking. For example, the way a hyena lifts its tail or stands can signal submission or dominance. Hyenas are also very vocal animals, using a range of sounds to communicate with one another. The most famous of these is their "laugh," which is actually a loud, high-pitched giggle-like sound that they make when they are excited or nervous. This laughing sound is often heard during feeding or when hyenas are in a conflict with other animals.

Speaking of feeding, one of the biggest myths about hyenas is that they are purely scavengers, meaning they only eat what other predators have killed. While it's true that hyenas will scavenge when they can, they are actually excellent hunters themselves. In fact, spotted hyenas are responsible for killing up to 95% of the food they eat! Hyenas are skilled, strategic hunters that often hunt in groups to bring down large prey like wildebeest or zebras. When hunting together, hyenas use teamwork to corner and exhaust their prey. Their endurance is impressive, as they can run long distances without getting tired, allowing them to chase down animals that are much bigger than they are. Hyenas are also highly adaptable, capable of hunting smaller animals like hares or birds when larger prey isn't available.

One of the reasons hyenas are so successful as hunters is because of their remarkable intelligence. Studies have shown that hyenas are among the most intelligent animals in the animal kingdom, rivaling primates like chimpanzees in problem-solving abilities. Their social structure requires them to understand complex relationships within their clan, and they have been observed working together to solve tasks that require teamwork and cooperation. Hyenas also have excellent memories, which help them remember the locations of food sources and the movements of other predators in their environment.

When hyenas hunt, they often clash with other predators like lions, leopards, and even wild dogs. There is a long-standing rivalry between lions and hyenas, as both species compete for the same prey. Hyenas and lions frequently steal food from each other, with battles breaking out over carcasses. Although lions are bigger and stronger, hyenas are clever and persistent. If they outnumber the lions, they can sometimes drive them away from a kill. Hyenas are also known for their ability to wait patiently for hours, watching and waiting for the right moment to swoop in and snatch food from a larger predator.

One of the most surprising things about hyenas is how well they take care of their young. Female spotted hyenas give birth in underground dens, where the cubs are kept safe from predators. Unlike many other animals, hyena mothers nurse their young for a long time—up to 18 months. During this time, the cubs grow strong on their mother's milk, which is very rich in nutrients. In fact, hyena milk is so nutritious that it helps the cubs grow quickly and gain strength faster than most other mammals. The cubs are born with their eyes open and with sharp teeth, which is unusual for many mammals. From the moment they are born, hyena cubs have to start figuring out their place in the clan's social structure, and sometimes they compete with their siblings for dominance.

Hyenas are also known for their impressive digestive systems. They are able to eat almost every part of an animal, including the bones, which they crush with their powerful jaws. Their stomachs can digest tough materials like bones, horns, and hooves, leaving almost nothing to waste. This ability to eat nearly anything allows hyenas to survive in harsh conditions where other predators might struggle to find food. In fact, hyenas are often the last animals feeding on a carcass, making sure that every bit of it is consumed.

Another fascinating aspect of hyenas is how they mark their territory. Hyenas have scent glands located under their tails, which produce a strong-smelling substance called "paste." They use this paste to mark the boundaries of their territory by rubbing it on grass, rocks, and trees. This scent tells other hyenas (and other animals) that the area belongs to their clan. By marking their territory, hyenas can avoid unnecessary fights with other clans over resources like food and water.

While hyenas may not have the regal reputation of lions or the majestic beauty of elephants, they play an essential role in the Serengeti ecosystem. As both hunters and scavengers, they help keep the balance of life in the Serengeti by controlling prey populations and cleaning up the remains of dead animals. Their ability to eat nearly anything means that they help prevent waste, making sure that every part of an animal is used. Without hyenas, the Serengeti would be a very different place, and the ecosystem could become unbalanced.

Hyenas also remind us that appearances can be deceiving. While they may not be as glamorous as some of the other animals in the Serengeti, they are intelligent, social, and incredibly adaptable creatures. They work together in their clans, hunt with skill and strategy, and take care of their young with dedication and care. Whether they're laughing, hunting, or protecting their territory, hyenas are full of surprises. The more we learn about them, the more we can appreciate their unique and important place in the Serengeti.

So, the next time you hear the cackle of a hyena or see one trotting across the plains, remember that there's so much more to these animals than meets the eye. They are survivors, problem-solvers, and key players in the Serengeti's story. Their hidden lives are filled with complex behaviors and incredible adaptations that make them one of the most remarkable animals in Africa. Hyenas may not always get the respect they deserve, but their intelligence, teamwork, and perseverance make them true champions of the wild.

Chapter 12: Crocodiles and Hippos in the Rivers

The rivers of the Serengeti are home to some of the most powerful and fascinating animals in the wild: crocodiles and hippos. These two massive creatures are masters of the water, and while they live in the same rivers, they have very different ways of life. Crocodiles and hippos are often seen together along the muddy riverbanks, yet they behave in such distinct ways that it's almost like watching two very different worlds. Despite their differences, both animals play important roles in the Serengeti's ecosystem, helping to keep the rivers alive with life and action. Their secretive and sometimes terrifying lives unfold beneath the surface of the water, where they swim, hunt, and guard their territories in ways that few get to see.

Let's begin with the crocodile, a creature that seems to have stepped right out of the age of the dinosaurs. Crocodiles have been around for over 200 million years, making them one of the oldest living species on Earth. In the Serengeti, the most common species is the Nile crocodile, and these reptiles are built to be perfect predators. They have long, muscular bodies covered in tough, scaly skin that acts like armor. Their strong, powerful tails help them swim quickly through the water, and their sharp teeth and strong jaws make them excellent hunters. When a crocodile closes its mouth, you can still see the sharp teeth sticking out, which gives them an even scarier appearance.

Crocodiles are known for their ability to stay almost completely hidden in the water. They can lie still for hours, with just their eyes and nostrils poking above the surface, waiting for the perfect moment to strike. Their camouflage is so good that prey animals like zebras or wildebeests often don't even realize they're there until it's too late. Crocodiles are ambush hunters, meaning they don't chase after their food. Instead, they wait patiently, sometimes for hours or even days, until an animal comes close enough for them to lunge out of the water and grab it. With their lightning-fast reflexes, they snap their powerful jaws around the animal, drag it into the water, and hold it under until it drowns.

One of the most dramatic moments in the life of a Serengeti crocodile happens during the Great Migration. Each year, millions of wildebeests and zebras make their way across the Serengeti in search of fresh grass to eat, and along the way, they must cross rivers. For the crocodiles, this is the perfect opportunity to catch a meal. As the herds approach the water, the crocodiles wait, still and silent, just beneath the surface. When the animals begin to cross the river, the crocodiles strike, creating a scene of chaos as they snatch prey from the water. It's a dangerous moment for the migrating animals, but for the crocodiles, it's a feast.

Crocodiles are not just hunters, though. They are also surprisingly attentive parents. Female crocodiles lay their eggs in nests made of mud and vegetation near the river's edge. After laying between 25 and 80 eggs, the mother crocodile will guard the nest fiercely, staying nearby to protect her young from predators like monitor lizards or birds. When the baby crocodiles are ready to hatch, they make chirping sounds from inside their eggs, and the mother will carefully dig them out of the nest and carry them to the water in her mouth. For the first few weeks of their lives, the baby crocodiles stay close to their mother, who continues to protect them until they are big enough to survive on their own.

On the other side of the river's ecosystem, we find the hippos, another giant of the Serengeti. Hippos may look slow and lazy as they lounge in the water, but they are actually one of the most dangerous animals in Africa. Despite their large, round bodies and short legs, hippos are incredibly strong and can run much faster than a human. They spend most of their day submerged in the water, where they stay cool under the hot African sun. Their thick skin can dry out and crack if they spend too much time on land, so the water is like a protective shield for them. Hippos are excellent swimmers and can hold their breath for up to five minutes, allowing them to move easily beneath the surface without being seen.

Hippos live in groups called pods, which can have anywhere from 10 to 30 members, although sometimes even larger groups can be found. The pod is usually led by a dominant male, who guards his territory fiercely. Male hippos are very territorial, especially in the water, and they will fight other males to defend their part of the river. These battles can be intense, with the males using their enormous mouths and sharp tusks to attack each other. Hippos have the largest mouths of any land animal, and they use them to make loud, deep grunts and roars that can be heard from miles away. These sounds are a way for hippos to communicate with each other and let others know where their territory is.

Even though hippos spend most of their time in the water, they are herbivores, meaning they only eat plants. At night, when it's cooler, hippos leave the water and walk long distances to find grass to graze on. They can eat up to 80 pounds of grass in a single night! Because of their size and strength, hippos don't have many natural predators, but young hippos can sometimes be threatened by lions or crocodiles. However, mother hippos are extremely protective of their babies, and few predators are brave enough to take on an adult hippo.

One of the most interesting things about hippos is how they interact with crocodiles. Even though they share the same rivers, hippos and crocodiles usually leave each other alone. In fact, hippos are so confident in their size and strength that they don't see crocodiles as a threat. Sometimes, you might even see hippos and crocodiles lying side by side on the riverbank, soaking up the sun. This unusual relationship is one of the many ways animals in the Serengeti learn to live together in balance, even when they are very different from each other.

However, things aren't always peaceful between these two giants of the river. If a crocodile gets too close to a young hippo, the mother hippo will attack. Hippos are much stronger than crocodiles and can easily injure or even kill them if they feel threatened. In some cases, hippos have been seen flipping crocodiles into the air with their powerful jaws to protect their young. Even adult crocodiles know better than to mess with a full-grown hippo.

The Serengeti's rivers are vital to both crocodiles and hippos, providing them with food, shelter, and a place to raise their young. But these rivers are not just important for the animals that live in them; they are also essential for the entire ecosystem. During the dry season, when water becomes scarce, animals from all over the Serengeti come to the rivers to drink. Crocodiles and hippos are part of the natural cycle that keeps the rivers healthy. Hippos help fertilize the water with their dung, which provides nutrients for fish and plants. Crocodiles, as both hunters and scavengers, help keep the rivers clean by eating dead animals that might otherwise pollute the water.

Despite their fearsome reputations, both crocodiles and hippos are vital to the balance of life in the Serengeti. Each one plays a unique role in the ecosystem, and without them, the rivers would not be the same. They are survivors of a wild and ancient world, where strength, patience, and adaptability are key. Watching them in the rivers of the Serengeti is like seeing nature at its most powerful and awe-inspiring. These massive creatures remind us of the untamed beauty of the wild, where life and death are always intertwined, and survival is never guaranteed.

In the end, the rivers of the Serengeti belong to both the crocodiles and the hippos, each dominating their own parts of the watery world. They may seem like opposites—one a sneaky, patient hunter, the other a loud and territorial giant—but both are masters of their environment. They share the rivers in a delicate balance, each with its own secrets, strengths, and stories to tell. For those lucky enough to witness them, crocodiles and hippos offer a glimpse into a world of ancient power and survival, where the hidden lives of these river giants unfold in ways that continue to amaze and inspire.

57

Chapter 13: Amazing Insects of the Serengeti

The Serengeti is not just about the big animals like lions, elephants, and giraffes. Beneath the tall grasses and the wide African skies, there's a whole world of tiny creatures that play an important role in the ecosystem. These amazing insects might be small, but they have some of the most fascinating stories to tell. From the buzzing bees to the colorful butterflies, and from the hardworking termites to the stealthy praying mantises, the Serengeti is full of insect life. Each of these creatures has its own unique way of surviving in this vast and wild land, and together, they make the Serengeti a much more interesting place.

One of the most well-known insects in the Serengeti is the honeybee. These buzzing insects are not only important for making delicious honey, but they also play a critical role in pollination. Pollination is the process of transferring pollen from one flower to another, which helps plants grow fruits and seeds. Without bees, many plants would not be able to reproduce. In the Serengeti, bees visit all kinds of flowers, from small, delicate wildflowers to large, bright-colored blooms. As they move from flower to flower, they spread pollen and help the plants thrive. This is especially important in the dry seasons when water is scarce, and every bit of plant life matters for the animals that rely on vegetation for food.

Bees are also part of a complex social system. They live in hives, where thousands of bees work together as a team. Inside the hive, there is one queen bee, who lays all the eggs. The worker bees, which are all female, gather nectar and pollen from flowers, build the hive, and take care of the baby bees, or larvae. The male bees, called drones, don't do much other than mate with the queen. Bees communicate with each other using a special dance. When a worker bee finds a good source of nectar, she returns to the hive and performs a "waggle dance," which tells the other bees exactly where to find the flowers. The life of a bee may seem simple, but it's actually full of teamwork, communication, and hard work.

But bees aren't the only pollinators in the Serengeti. Butterflies, with their bright colors and delicate wings, are also important for spreading pollen. There are many different species of butterflies in the Serengeti, each with its own patterns and colors. Some butterflies are orange and black, while others have blue, yellow, or even white wings. Butterflies spend their days fluttering from flower to flower, drinking nectar and helping to spread pollen. What's really amazing about butterflies is their life cycle. They start as tiny eggs laid on the leaves of plants. When the eggs hatch, the larvae, or caterpillars, emerge. These caterpillars spend their time munching on leaves, growing bigger and bigger. After a while, the caterpillar wraps itself in a protective shell called a chrysalis. Inside the chrysalis, something incredible happens—the caterpillar transforms into a butterfly. This process, called metamorphosis, is one of the most magical transformations in nature.

While butterflies and bees may be the most noticeable insects in the Serengeti, some of the most important work is done by creatures that are much less glamorous: termites. Termites are tiny, pale insects that live in huge colonies, sometimes numbering in the millions. They build massive mounds out of mud, saliva, and dung, which can rise several feet above the ground. These mounds are not just homes for the termites—they are engineering marvels. Inside the mound, termites create a network of tunnels and chambers that help regulate the temperature and humidity, keeping the environment just right for the colony.

Termites are known as decomposers because they feed on dead plant material, such as wood, grass, and leaves. As they break down this material, they help return nutrients to the soil, which allows plants to grow. Without termites, the Serengeti's ecosystem would struggle to stay healthy, as dead plants would pile up and the soil would become less fertile. In fact, termites are so important that they are often called the "engineers of the ecosystem." Even though they are tiny and not very impressive to look at, termites have a huge impact on the land.

While termites are busy decomposing plant material, another insect is working hard in a very different way. The dung beetle has a rather dirty job, but it's one of the most important in the Serengeti. Dung beetles, as their name suggests, feed on animal dung. When a large animal like an elephant or buffalo leaves behind its droppings, dung beetles rush to the scene. They roll the dung into small balls and bury them in the ground. The beetles then lay their eggs in the dung, which provides food for their larvae when they hatch. This process helps keep the Serengeti clean by breaking down the dung and returning nutrients to the soil, much like the work termites do with dead plants.

Dung beetles are surprisingly strong for their size. Some species can roll dung balls that are up to 50 times their own weight! Imagine being able to push something that weighs as much as a car—that's how strong these little beetles are. Watching a dung beetle roll a perfectly round ball of dung across the ground is a strange but fascinating sight, and it's one of the many ways insects help maintain balance in the Serengeti.

Another fascinating insect in the Serengeti is the praying mantis. This insect is a master of camouflage and stealth, using its leaf-like appearance to hide among the plants. The praying mantis is a predator, feeding on other insects like flies, grasshoppers, and even butterflies. Its long front legs are specially designed for catching prey. When a mantis spots a potential meal, it stays perfectly still, waiting for the right moment to strike. Then, with lightning speed, it grabs the insect with its sharp legs and starts to eat. The mantis is so quick that its movements are often too fast to see with the naked eye.

The praying mantis gets its name from the way it holds its front legs, as if it's in a prayer position. But don't let its peaceful appearance fool you—this insect is a fierce hunter. Female praying mantises are known for sometimes eating the male after mating, a behavior that might seem shocking but is common in the insect world. Despite this, praying mantises are beneficial to the ecosystem because they help control the population of other insects, keeping everything in balance.

No discussion of insects in the Serengeti would be complete without mentioning the tsetse fly. This tiny insect may not look very dangerous, but it is responsible for spreading a disease called sleeping sickness, which affects both animals and humans. The tsetse fly feeds on the blood of mammals, and when it bites, it can pass on the parasites that cause sleeping sickness. For animals like cattle, horses, and even some wild species, sleeping sickness can be deadly. This is why tsetse flies are one of the most feared insects in the Serengeti.

However, even tsetse flies have their place in the ecosystem. Their presence can limit the spread of human settlements in certain areas, helping to preserve the natural habitats of wild animals. While they may cause harm, they also remind us of the delicate balance that exists in nature, where every creature, no matter how small or annoying, plays a part in the bigger picture.

Among the Serengeti's many insects, ants are another group that deserves attention. There are thousands of species of ants, and they can be found almost everywhere in the Serengeti. Some ants live in colonies underground, while others build nests in trees or under rocks. Ants are incredibly strong for their size and can carry objects many times their own weight. They work together in highly organized groups, with each ant having a specific job to do, whether it's gathering food, taking care of the young, or defending the colony.

One of the most interesting species of ants in the Serengeti is the driver ant, also known as the safari ant. These ants live in huge colonies and are known for their aggressive behavior. When driver ants are on the move, they travel in massive groups, attacking anything in their path. They are fearless and will take down insects, small animals, and even larger creatures if they get in the way. Watching a swarm of driver ants march across the ground is an incredible sight, as they seem to move with one mind, all working together to find food and protect their colony.

Even though they are small, insects play a huge role in the Serengeti. They may not get as much attention as the larger animals, but without them, the entire ecosystem would struggle to survive. Insects like bees, butterflies, termites, dung beetles, praying mantises, tsetse flies, and ants all have important jobs to do, from pollinating plants to cleaning up waste to controlling other insect populations. Each insect is a tiny piece of a much bigger puzzle, and together, they help keep the Serengeti healthy and thriving.

The amazing insects of the Serengeti remind us that even the smallest creatures can have a big impact on the world around them. Whether they're buzzing through the air, crawling through the grass, or building intricate underground colonies, these insects are an essential part of life in this vast and beautiful land. They might not be as fierce as lions or as majestic as elephants, but without them, the Serengeti would not be the incredible, diverse ecosystem that it is today.

Chapter 14: How Maasai People Live with Wildlife

The Maasai people are one of the most famous and fascinating tribes in Africa, and they have lived in harmony with wildlife for hundreds of years. Their homeland stretches across the vast plains of Kenya and Tanzania, right in the heart of the Serengeti region. The Maasai are known for their rich culture, colorful clothing, and unique way of life, but what makes them truly special is how they have learned to coexist with the wild animals that roam these lands. Living among lions, elephants, giraffes, zebras, and many other creatures, the Maasai have developed a deep respect for nature and its inhabitants. Understanding how the Maasai people live with wildlife can give us a glimpse into a way of life that values balance, tradition, and respect for all living things.

For the Maasai, the land they live on is not just a place to build homes and graze cattle; it is a sacred space that they believe is shared with the animals. The Maasai have always seen themselves as caretakers of the land, responsible for protecting it and the creatures that call it home. One of the ways they do this is by living a semi-nomadic lifestyle. This means that they move their cattle, which are their most important source of livelihood, from place to place in search of fresh grazing land. By moving around, they prevent overgrazing and allow the land to recover, which helps maintain a healthy environment for both their cattle and the wildlife that live there.

Cattle are central to Maasai life. The Maasai measure wealth in terms of how many cattle a person owns, and they rely on their cows for milk, which is a major part of their diet. They rarely slaughter cattle for meat, as they consider the animals too valuable. Instead, they prefer to live off milk, blood (taken from the cow without killing it), and sometimes a little meat from goats or sheep. Because of this, the Maasai people have developed a way of life that depends on their cattle but does not harm the wildlife around them. In fact, they often graze their herds in areas where wild animals live, allowing both domestic and wild animals to share the same land.

Despite living so closely with wildlife, the Maasai have learned to avoid conflict with dangerous animals like lions and elephants. Instead of fearing them, the Maasai have developed clever ways to protect themselves and their livestock. For example, when it comes to lions, the Maasai are known for their bravery. In the past, young Maasai warriors, known as morans, would prove their courage by hunting lions. However, this was not done out of hatred or the desire to kill but as a test of strength and bravery. In modern times, lion hunting has mostly stopped, as the Maasai have come to realize the importance of preserving these majestic creatures. Instead, the Maasai now focus on protecting their cattle from lions by building strong enclosures called bomas, made of thorny bushes and sturdy fences, to keep the predators out at night.

The Maasai also use traditional knowledge to avoid encounters with elephants. Elephants are known to raid crops and sometimes damage villages, but the Maasai have learned to live with them peacefully. One way they do this is by keeping their settlements away from known elephant paths. Elephants tend to use the same routes to travel from one place to another, so the Maasai make sure to avoid these areas when setting up their homes. Additionally, the Maasai have learned that elephants dislike the smell of certain plants, so they sometimes plant these around their villages to keep the giants away.

Perhaps one of the most remarkable things about the Maasai is their deep respect for the wildlife around them. They believe that animals have as much right to the land as they do, and they often see the presence of animals as a blessing. For the Maasai, animals like lions, elephants, and even small creatures are all part of the natural world that must be protected. This respect for animals is deeply rooted in their culture and beliefs. They view the land and its creatures as gifts from their god, Enkai, and they take their role as stewards of the land seriously.

Another interesting aspect of Maasai life is how they have adapted to modern conservation efforts. In recent years, many Maasai communities have become involved in wildlife conservation projects. This is partly because they understand the importance of protecting the Serengeti and its wildlife for future generations. Some Maasai have even become park rangers or guides, helping tourists experience the beauty of the Serengeti while teaching them about the importance of conservation. These efforts not only protect the animals but also provide income for Maasai communities, allowing them to maintain their traditional way of life while benefiting from modern tourism.

The Maasai have also embraced wildlife conservation in more personal ways. One of the most exciting projects is the Maasai-led Lion Guardians program. This program was created to help protect lions while reducing conflict between the Maasai and these big cats. Instead of hunting lions, Maasai warriors now work to track and monitor them. The Lion Guardians use traditional Maasai knowledge of the land and animals to follow lions' movements and protect both the lions and the Maasai cattle. This project has been incredibly successful, reducing the number of lions killed and strengthening the relationship between the Maasai and the wildlife they live alongside.

The Maasai's respect for nature is not just about big animals like lions and elephants. They also understand the importance of smaller creatures, like birds and insects, in maintaining the balance of the ecosystem. The Maasai often observe the behavior of birds to predict changes in the weather or to find water sources. They know that when certain birds gather in large numbers or fly in specific directions, it can mean that rain is coming or that there is water nearby. This knowledge has been passed down from generation to generation and is an important part of how the Maasai live in harmony with their environment.

In Maasai culture, everything is connected. They believe that people, animals, plants, and the land are all part of the same great circle of life. This belief influences how they treat the environment and how they interact with the wildlife around them. The Maasai do not take more from the land than they need, and they always try to give back in some way, whether by protecting the land, conserving water, or sharing their knowledge with others. This attitude has allowed them to live sustainably in the Serengeti for centuries, even as the world around them changes.

Of course, the Maasai way of life is not without its challenges. As human populations grow and more land is needed for farming and development, the Maasai's traditional lands are shrinking. This has made it harder for them to live as they once did, moving their cattle freely across the plains. Additionally, climate change is causing longer dry seasons and less reliable rainfall, making it difficult to find enough water and grazing land for their cattle. Despite these challenges, the Maasai are finding ways to adapt while still holding on to their traditions.

One of the ways the Maasai are adapting is by becoming involved in community-based tourism. Some Maasai villages have opened their doors to visitors, offering tourists the chance to learn about their culture and way of life. Tourists can visit Maasai homesteads, called manyattas, where they can see traditional dances, learn about Maasai customs, and even take part in activities like milking cows or building bomas. This type of tourism helps to support Maasai communities financially while also educating people about the importance of conserving the Serengeti's wildlife and respecting local cultures.

The Maasai have also begun to explore new ways of managing their cattle to reduce their impact on the environment. Some communities are experimenting with rotational grazing, where cattle are moved from one area to another in a more organized way. This helps to prevent overgrazing and allows the land to recover, ensuring that both cattle and wildlife have enough food. By combining traditional knowledge with modern techniques, the Maasai are finding ways to protect the land they love while still maintaining their connection to it.

In the end, the Maasai people are a living example of how humans can live in harmony with wildlife. Their deep respect for nature, combined with their ability to adapt to changing circumstances, has allowed them to thrive in one of the most beautiful and wild places on Earth. The Maasai's way of life reminds us that we are all part of the same natural world and that by respecting and protecting the animals and the environment, we can create a better future for everyone.

Chapter 15: The Changing Seasons of the Serengeti

The Serengeti is one of the most amazing places on Earth, not just because of the incredible animals that live there but also because of the way its landscape transforms with the changing seasons. The Serengeti, which means "endless plains" in the Maasai language, covers about 30,000 square kilometers (12,000 square miles) of land across Tanzania and Kenya. This vast stretch of land is home to grasslands, woodlands, rivers, and kopjes (rocky outcrops), all of which change dramatically as the seasons shift. The animals and plants of the Serengeti must adapt to these changes, and understanding the Serengeti's seasons helps explain the behavior and survival strategies of the animals that live there.

In the Serengeti, there are two main seasons: the wet season and the dry season. These two periods shape everything in the ecosystem. The rainy season lasts from about November to May, while the dry season occurs from June to October. Each season brings its own unique challenges and opportunities for the animals and plants that live there.

When the rains begin in November, the Serengeti transforms into a lush, green paradise. After months of dry, dusty conditions, the ground finally receives the water it needs, and plants spring to life. Grasses grow tall and green, and the acacia trees burst with fresh leaves. The rivers and watering holes, which may have nearly dried up during the dry season, fill with water again, providing a lifeline for animals.

During the wet season, the Serengeti becomes a place of abundance. For herbivores like zebras, wildebeest, and gazelles, the wet season is the best time of the year. The fresh grass and leaves provide plenty of food for them to graze on. These animals travel across the plains in search of the best grazing areas, but they don't have to travel as far as they do during the dry season, because food and water are plentiful everywhere. The wet season is also the time when many animals give birth. The abundance of food makes it easier for mothers to feed their young, and the lush vegetation provides some cover from predators.

However, the wet season also brings challenges. With the rains come floods, and some parts of the Serengeti can become difficult to navigate due to the waterlogged ground. The rivers, now swollen with rainwater, can be dangerous to cross. For animals like wildebeest, zebras, and gazelles, crossing rivers is a necessary but risky task. Crocodiles lie in wait in the water, ready to strike as the herds make their way across.

The predators of the Serengeti, like lions, leopards, cheetahs, and hyenas, also take advantage of the abundance of prey during the wet season. With so many young animals being born, it's a time of plenty for these carnivores. The tall grasses and thick vegetation make it easier for predators to hide as they stalk their prey. Lions and leopards, in particular, rely on stealth to hunt, and the lush greenery provides excellent cover for them as they creep up on unsuspecting herds.

As the wet season continues, the Serengeti thrives. Birds are abundant, from the towering ostriches to the colorful lilac-breasted rollers. The wetlands and rivers are full of life, with hippos wallowing in the water and fish thriving in the newly replenished rivers. Insects, too, are everywhere, providing food for birds and small mammals. Everything seems to be alive and flourishing during the rains.

But, all good things must come to an end. By May, the rains start to slow down, and the dry season begins to take hold. As the wet season gives way to the dry season, the Serengeti undergoes a dramatic transformation. The once-lush grasslands start to turn brown and dry. The rivers and waterholes begin to shrink, and the landscape takes on a harsher, more arid appearance.

For the animals of the Serengeti, the dry season is a time of scarcity. Water becomes harder to find, and the grass that was once plentiful is now dry and brittle. Herbivores must travel long distances in search of food and water, often following ancient migratory routes that take them from one part of the Serengeti to another. This is the time when the Great Migration occurs. Over a million wildebeest, accompanied by hundreds of thousands of zebras and gazelles, travel across the Serengeti and into the neighboring Maasai Mara in Kenya in search of greener pastures. The migration is one of the most spectacular wildlife events on the planet, as these animals move in massive herds, following the rains to find food.

During the dry season, life becomes more challenging for all of the Serengeti's inhabitants. The shrinking water sources become gathering spots for animals, which makes them dangerous places. As herds of zebras, wildebeest, and gazelles come to drink, predators like lions, leopards, and crocodiles wait nearby, ready to pounce. The competition for food and water is fierce during this time, and only the strongest animals survive.

Elephants, with their incredible strength and intelligence, are some of the best-equipped animals to handle the dry season. They can dig into dry riverbeds with their tusks to create waterholes, providing water for themselves and other animals. Elephants also have the ability to travel long distances in search of water, and they use their large ears to cool themselves down in the scorching heat. Giraffes, too, have adapted well to the dry season, as they can eat the leaves of acacia trees, which remain green even when the grass has dried up.

The dry season is also a time of great opportunity for predators. With fewer places for prey to hide, lions, leopards, cheetahs, and hyenas have an easier time spotting their targets. The dry grasslands offer little cover for zebras and wildebeest, making them more vulnerable to attacks. For the predators, the dry season is a time when they can feast, but for the herbivores, it is a time of constant vigilance and danger.

The dry season can be particularly hard on young animals. Without the abundance of food and water that the wet season provides, many young herbivores struggle to survive. Predators take advantage of this, targeting the weak and vulnerable. However, the dry season is also a time when the strongest animals prove their resilience. Those that can survive the long months of drought will be rewarded when the rains return.

As the dry season reaches its peak in September and October, the Serengeti becomes a harsh, dusty place. The rivers have shrunk to a fraction of their size, and the grasslands are brown and parched. Dust storms can sweep across the plains, and the sun beats down relentlessly. But even in this difficult time, life goes on. The animals of the Serengeti have evolved over millions of years to survive these tough conditions, and they have developed incredible adaptations to cope with the heat and lack of water.

Finally, as October draws to a close, the skies begin to darken with heavy clouds, and the first signs of the wet season return. The cycle begins anew, as the rains bring life back to the Serengeti. The brown, dry grasslands start to turn green again, and the rivers fill with water. The animals, too, begin to move in response to the changing conditions. The Great Migration reverses course, as the herds return to the Serengeti to take advantage of the fresh grass. New life is born, and the Serengeti becomes a place of abundance once again.

The changing seasons of the Serengeti are a reminder of the incredible balance of nature. Each season brings its own challenges and opportunities, and the animals of the Serengeti have learned to adapt to these changes in remarkable ways. The Serengeti is a place where life is constantly in motion, where the rains bring life and the dry season tests the strength of every creature. It's a place of beauty and survival, where the cycle of life continues year after year, just as it has for millions of years. The Serengeti's seasons are more than just weather patterns; they are the heartbeat of one of the wildest, most incredible places on Earth.

Chapter 16: Exploring the Serengeti's Acacia Trees

The Serengeti is known for its vast, open plains, but it's also home to some very special trees that play a big role in the ecosystem—the acacia trees. These trees are not just any ordinary trees; they are a key part of the landscape, providing food, shelter, and protection to a wide range of animals and insects. Exploring the Serengeti's acacia trees is like unlocking a hidden world of interactions between plants, animals, and the environment, each depending on the other in ways that may not be obvious at first glance. The acacia tree might look simple with its thorny branches and umbrella-like shape, but when you look closely, you'll discover how vital these trees are to the Serengeti.

Acacia trees are iconic across Africa, especially in the Serengeti. They are easily recognized by their flat tops and thorn-covered branches. These trees can grow tall, some reaching up to 20 meters (about 66 feet) in height, and they are spread across the landscape like green islands in a sea of golden grass. Acacias are well-adapted to the tough conditions of the Serengeti, where water can be scarce for much of the year. Their deep roots allow them to access water far below the surface, and their small, waxy leaves help them conserve moisture during the dry season.

But acacia trees are more than just survivors in a harsh environment—they are essential to the animals that live around them. For herbivores like giraffes, zebras, and elephants, acacias are a critical source of food. Giraffes, with their long necks and tongues, are especially fond of acacia leaves, despite the trees' thorny defenses. They have adapted to pluck the leaves delicately from between the thorns using their prehensile tongues, which are rough and tough enough to avoid being hurt by the sharp spikes. You might think the acacia trees wouldn't want their leaves eaten, but in fact, they have developed a relationship with the animals. In some cases, herbivores like giraffes help the tree by trimming its leaves, which encourages new growth. It's a balance between giving and taking—giraffes get the food they need, and the acacia trees stay healthy by sprouting fresh leaves.

However, acacia trees aren't just passive participants in this relationship. They have developed clever ways to protect themselves from being overeaten. When a giraffe starts nibbling on an acacia tree, the tree reacts by releasing a chemical called tannin into its leaves. Tannin makes the leaves taste bitter and can even make it harder for animals to digest them. But that's not all—acacia trees can also send out signals to other trees nearby. When one tree is being eaten, it releases a gas called ethylene, which warns other acacia trees in the area to start producing tannins in their leaves, making them less appetizing to the hungry giraffes or other herbivores.

Elephants also have a strong connection to the acacia trees of the Serengeti. These large animals are known for their powerful trunks and ability to knock down trees when they want to get to the leaves or bark. For acacia trees, this might seem like a bad thing, but it's part of the natural cycle. When elephants push over or break acacia trees, they open up space in the landscape, allowing sunlight to reach the ground and encouraging new plants to grow. This creates a more diverse environment where smaller plants can thrive, benefiting other animals like antelopes and zebras that prefer to graze on grasses rather than browse on leaves.

Acacia trees are also home to a variety of birds and insects. The umbrella-like shape of the tree creates the perfect spot for birds to build their nests. Weaver birds, for instance, are known for their intricate nests, which they construct by weaving grass and twigs together. These birds prefer to nest in acacia trees because the thorns help protect them from predators like snakes or larger birds. The nests of weaver birds can often be seen hanging from the branches of acacia trees, swaying gently in the breeze. Other birds, such as hornbills and eagles, also make their homes in the acacia trees, taking advantage of the high vantage point to spot prey or keep watch for danger.

Insects, too, have a special relationship with acacia trees. Perhaps the most fascinating of these are the ants that live in the acacia's thorns. Some species of acacia trees have hollow thorns that serve as homes for ants. In exchange for a safe place to live, the ants protect the acacia tree from herbivores. When an animal like a giraffe or elephant starts to eat the tree's leaves, the ants swarm out of the thorns and bite the intruder, driving it away. This mutualistic relationship benefits both the acacia tree and the ants—the tree gets protection from being eaten, and the ants get a safe, stable home inside the thorny branches.

The acacia's flowers are another important part of the tree's life cycle. These small, white or yellow blossoms appear during the rainy season and are rich in nectar. They attract bees, butterflies, and other pollinators, which help the acacia tree reproduce by transferring pollen from one flower to another. Pollination is essential for the acacia tree to produce seeds, which will eventually grow into new trees. In this way, the acacia tree ensures the survival of its species while also providing food for the insects that visit its flowers.

When the dry season comes, the acacia tree's role in the ecosystem becomes even more important. As water sources dry up and the grasslands turn brown, the acacia trees remain green, providing a vital source of food for animals that depend on them. The deep roots of the acacia tree allow it to tap into underground water, keeping it alive even during long periods of drought. This resilience makes acacia trees a reliable food source for herbivores like giraffes, elephants, and gazelles during the toughest times of the year. Even when the ground is parched and most plants have withered, the acacia tree stands tall, its leaves offering life-giving nourishment to the animals that rely on it.

Acacia trees are also an important part of the Serengeti's nutrient cycle. When the leaves, flowers, or branches of an acacia tree fall to the ground, they decompose and return nutrients to the soil. This process enriches the earth, allowing new plants to grow. In this way, acacia trees help to maintain the fertility of the Serengeti's soil, supporting the growth of grasses and other vegetation that animals need to survive. Even in death, the acacia tree plays a crucial role in the ecosystem, contributing to the cycle of life in the Serengeti.

The presence of acacia trees in the Serengeti also influences the behavior of other animals. For example, cheetahs and lions often use acacia trees as resting spots or lookout points. The shade provided by the tree's wide canopy offers relief from the intense heat of the African sun, while the height of the tree allows predators to scan the horizon for prey. Acacia trees are also used as landmarks by animals migrating across the plains. These trees stand out in the otherwise open landscape, making them important reference points for animals as they navigate the vast Serengeti.

Even humans have learned to live alongside acacia trees. The Maasai people, who have lived in the Serengeti for centuries, use acacia wood to build their homes and thorny branches to create protective fences around their villages. The acacia tree's significance in Maasai culture is a testament to its importance not just to animals, but to people as well.

Exploring the Serengeti's acacia trees reveals a world of intricate relationships and interdependencies. These trees are not only a source of food and shelter but also play a central role in the survival of countless species in the Serengeti. From the towering giraffes that graze on their leaves to the tiny ants that defend them from harm, the acacia tree is at the heart of life on the African plains. Without acacia trees, the Serengeti would be a very different place, and the delicate balance of its ecosystem would be disrupted. So, the next time you see an acacia tree standing proudly in the Serengeti, remember that it's not just a tree—it's a symbol of life, resilience, and the remarkable connections that exist in the wild.

Chapter 17: The Role of Rangers in Protecting Wildlife

Rangers play an essential role in protecting wildlife, especially in places like the Serengeti, where vast numbers of animals roam freely across wide landscapes. Their work is crucial in keeping the balance of nature intact and ensuring that future generations can continue to enjoy the incredible beauty of the natural world. But their job is far more than just watching over animals. Rangers are the unseen guardians of wildlife, working behind the scenes to protect the creatures of the Serengeti from numerous threats. They face challenges every day, but their dedication to preserving wildlife is what makes them such important figures in the conservation world.

One of the main responsibilities of rangers is to protect animals from poachers. Poaching, the illegal hunting of animals, is one of the biggest dangers to wildlife, particularly in places like the Serengeti. Poachers often target animals like elephants, rhinos, and big cats for their valuable parts, such as tusks, horns, or pelts, which can be sold for large sums of money on the black market. Rangers patrol vast areas of land to stop these poachers from harming the animals. It's a difficult and dangerous job, but without the presence of rangers, poaching could quickly spiral out of control, and many of the animals we love could be wiped out forever.

Rangers usually work in teams, covering the vast stretches of the Serengeti on foot, in vehicles, or sometimes even on horseback. They have to be highly trained in many different skills. They learn how to track animals by looking for footprints, droppings, or signs like broken branches, all clues that help them understand where animals have been and where they are going. But they also learn how to track poachers, spotting signs that humans have been in areas they shouldn't be. This could be anything from footprints to campsites, or even small items left behind, like cigarette butts. Rangers must be sharp-eyed and able to think like both an animal and a poacher to keep ahead of those who wish to harm the wildlife.

Stopping poachers isn't just about catching them in the act; it's also about preventing poaching from happening in the first place. Rangers often set up anti-poaching patrols and create roadblocks to check for suspicious activity. They use advanced technology like drones and GPS to monitor large areas and keep an eye on animal movements. Some rangers even use sniffer dogs, specially trained to detect animal parts like ivory or rhino horn. These dogs can smell things that humans would never be able to detect, making them valuable partners in the fight against poaching. Thanks to these strategies, rangers are able to prevent many illegal activities before they can even begin.

However, protecting animals from poachers is just one part of a ranger's job. They also work to conserve the entire ecosystem of the Serengeti. This means protecting not just the animals, but the plants, rivers, and landscapes that all living creatures depend on. Rangers monitor the health of the environment, checking for signs of problems like soil erosion, deforestation, or pollution. If the grasslands of the Serengeti become damaged, the animals won't have enough food to survive, so rangers take steps to make sure that the land remains healthy. This might involve planting trees, managing water sources, or controlling fires that could spread and destroy habitats.

Rangers also have an important role in managing human-wildlife conflict. In places like the Serengeti, where animals and people live close to each other, there can be conflicts when animals like elephants or lions wander into areas where people are living or farming. Elephants, for example, might trample crops, and lions might attack livestock like cows or goats. When this happens, people sometimes retaliate by trying to kill the animals to protect their livelihoods. Rangers work with local communities to find solutions to these problems. They teach people how to protect their crops and livestock without harming the animals. Sometimes they build strong fences or use techniques like bee hives, as elephants are afraid of bees and will avoid areas where they are present. By helping people and animals live together peacefully, rangers reduce the chances of animals being harmed.

Another key role that rangers play is in education. They often work with local communities, schools, and tourists to teach them about the importance of wildlife conservation. Many people in nearby villages may not fully understand why it's so important to protect animals like elephants, rhinos, or lions. By educating people, rangers help create a culture of conservation where everyone plays a role in protecting the wildlife. This is especially important for the younger generation, as children who grow up understanding the value of wildlife are more likely to become protectors of nature in the future. Rangers give talks, lead tours, and organize community events to spread the message of conservation far and wide.

Tourism is another area where rangers make a big impact. The Serengeti is a world-famous destination, with people traveling from all over the globe to see the incredible wildlife. Rangers often serve as guides, taking visitors on safaris and sharing their deep knowledge about the animals and ecosystems of the Serengeti. Their work helps tourists appreciate the beauty and importance of wildlife, while also ensuring that tourism is conducted in a way that doesn't harm the environment. They enforce rules about keeping a safe distance from animals, not disturbing their natural behaviors, and respecting the land. The money generated from tourism often goes back into funding conservation efforts, so rangers play a key part in making sure that wildlife protection is sustainable.

In addition to their work with animals and people, rangers have to keep themselves prepared for the physical challenges of the job. The Serengeti is a tough place to work, with extreme heat, long hours, and sometimes dangerous animals. Rangers are often out on patrols for days at a time, sleeping in the wilderness and surviving with only the supplies they can carry with them. They need to be in excellent physical shape, able to hike long distances, and respond quickly to emergencies. Whether it's rescuing an injured animal or responding to a poaching alert, rangers have to be ready for anything. Their work is not easy, but their passion for wildlife keeps them going, no matter how tough the conditions might be.

Many people see rangers as heroes, and rightfully so. Without them, many of the animals that call the Serengeti home would be in danger of extinction. Elephants, lions, rhinos, and other animals would be much more vulnerable to poachers, and the delicate balance of the Serengeti ecosystem could be lost. Rangers are often the last line of defense between the animals and the threats that surround them, and their efforts are vital in maintaining the health and safety of the environment. They are the unsung protectors of the wild, working tirelessly to ensure that animals can continue to roam free across the plains of the Serengeti.

In many cases, rangers form deep bonds with the wildlife they protect. They might recognize individual animals and watch over them for years, knowing their patterns, families, and even personalities. For some rangers, their work is more than just a job—it's a calling. They feel a strong connection to the land and the creatures that live on it, dedicating their lives to the cause of conservation. These bonds are what make the job so rewarding, as rangers get to see the results of their hard work every day. Knowing that they are helping to save endangered species and protect the environment gives rangers a sense of purpose and pride.

Despite the dangers and challenges, rangers remain dedicated to their mission of protecting the Serengeti's wildlife. Whether they are stopping poachers, educating communities, or ensuring that the ecosystem remains healthy, rangers are a crucial part of the conservation effort. Their work helps preserve the rich biodiversity of the Serengeti, ensuring that future generations can continue to marvel at the incredible animals and landscapes that make this place so special. Thanks to the tireless efforts of rangers, the Serengeti remains a haven for wildlife, a place where the natural world thrives, and where the delicate balance of nature is carefully maintained.

Chapter 18: How Climate Shapes the Serengeti

The climate of the Serengeti plays a huge role in shaping everything that lives in this incredible landscape, from the tallest trees to the tiniest insects, and of course, the animals that roam its plains. The weather patterns here are not just something you notice in the sky—they control the movement of animals, the growth of plants, and even how people live in and around the area. To truly understand the Serengeti, you have to know how its climate works and how it influences every aspect of life in this world-famous ecosystem.

The Serengeti has a tropical climate, but it's not the kind of tropical weather where it rains all the time or stays hot year-round. Instead, it's marked by two distinct seasons: the wet season and the dry season. Each of these seasons brings its own challenges and opportunities for the animals and plants that call the Serengeti home. The wet season usually lasts from November to May, and it's the time when the Serengeti is transformed into a lush, green paradise. During this period, rain showers sweep across the land, turning the dry, dusty plains into rich fields of grass. This grass becomes a crucial source of food for many of the animals that live here, particularly herbivores like zebras, wildebeest, and gazelles. These animals rely on the rains to nourish the plants they eat, and when the rains come, it signals the start of a season of plenty for them.

But the wet season doesn't just bring food; it also brings life in other ways. Many animals in the Serengeti time the birth of their young to coincide with the rains. This is because the abundance of fresh grass and water makes it easier for mothers to feed their babies. Wildebeest, for example, give birth in massive numbers during the wet season, and for a few weeks, the plains are filled with thousands of tiny calves learning to walk and run. It's a sight to behold—an explosion of new life, all made possible by the rainfall. For predators like lions and hyenas, this is also a good time, as the young herbivores make easy prey while they are still learning how to avoid danger.

However, the wet season is not all easy living. The heavy rains can sometimes make the ground soggy and muddy, making it harder for some animals to move around. Rivers and lakes swell with the extra water, and in some cases, animals have to deal with flooding or getting stuck in muddy areas. The rains also bring out a lot of insects, some of which can be bothersome to the larger animals. Mosquitoes and tsetse flies, for example, thrive in the wet conditions and can be a nuisance to both animals and humans. But despite these challenges, most creatures of the Serengeti flourish during the wet season, as the rain brings much-needed life to the land.

As the wet season comes to an end, the Serengeti begins to prepare for the dry season, which typically lasts from June to October. This is when the climate starts to really shape how animals behave. The rain stops, and the hot sun begins to dry up the water sources, causing the grass to wither and the rivers to shrink. As the landscape turns from green to brown, the animals have to adapt to the changing conditions. For many herbivores, this means moving in search of fresh grass and water, which is why the Great Migration takes place. Wildebeest, zebras, and gazelles travel hundreds of miles during the dry season, following the rains and the green grass they bring. This migration is one of the most famous events in the animal kingdom, and it wouldn't happen without the Serengeti's distinct climate.

For animals that don't migrate, the dry season can be a tough time. Water becomes scarce, and the grass they rely on for food becomes harder to find. Elephants, for example, are known to dig into dry riverbeds with their trunks to find water hidden beneath the surface. They'll also use their powerful trunks to strip bark from trees, as the bark contains moisture and nutrients that can help them survive when there's little grass. Giraffes, with their long necks, can reach the leaves of tall trees, which helps them during the dry season when food on the ground is scarce.

Predators like lions, cheetahs, and leopards also feel the effects of the dry season, but in a different way. As the herbivores move in search of water, predators have to follow them. This means that lions and other carnivores often travel longer distances to find prey. However, the dry season can also work in the predators' favor. With less water around, animals gather in large numbers at the remaining water sources, making it easier for predators to find and hunt them. Crocodiles, in particular, take advantage of this, lying in wait near shrinking rivers and waterholes, ready to snap at any animal that comes too close.

The Serengeti's dry season is also when fires can break out. These fires are usually caused by lightning strikes during the early part of the dry season, and while they might seem destructive, they actually play an important role in the ecosystem. Fires clear away dead grass and plants, making room for new growth when the rains return. They also help control the population of certain plant species, preventing them from taking over the landscape. In this way, the Serengeti's climate, with its dry spells and occasional fires, helps maintain the balance of the ecosystem.

But climate doesn't just affect animals—it shapes the entire Serengeti landscape. The grasses of the Serengeti have adapted to survive the changing seasons, growing quickly during the wet season and becoming dormant during the dry season. Acacia trees, which are a common sight across the plains, have deep roots that allow them to reach water even during the driest months. These trees provide shade and food for many animals, especially giraffes and elephants. The Serengeti's plants have evolved over millions of years to withstand the extremes of its climate, making them just as resilient as the animals that depend on them.

The people who live in and around the Serengeti, such as the Maasai, have also learned to adapt to the climate. For centuries, the Maasai have herded cattle across the plains, following the same patterns of movement as the animals. They know when to move their herds to find fresh grass and water, and they have developed a deep understanding of how the climate shapes the land. Their way of life is closely connected to the rhythm of the seasons, and like the animals of the Serengeti, they rely on the rain to sustain their herds and provide for their families.

In recent years, the Serengeti's climate has become more unpredictable due to climate change. Some years, the rains come later or are shorter than usual, while in other years, there might be too much rain, leading to floods. These changes in the climate are challenging for both the animals and the people who live in the Serengeti. If the wet season becomes too short, the grass may not grow enough to feed the millions of herbivores, which could have a ripple effect on the entire ecosystem. Similarly, if the dry season becomes longer, water sources may disappear completely, forcing animals to migrate even farther in search of food and water.

Conservationists are working to understand how climate change is affecting the Serengeti and what can be done to protect its unique ecosystem. Rangers, scientists, and local communities are coming together to find solutions, such as creating protected areas where animals can find food and water even during times of drought. These efforts are crucial in helping the Serengeti adapt to the changing climate and ensuring that it remains a haven for wildlife for generations to come.

In conclusion, the climate of the Serengeti is more than just a backdrop to the action—it's a driving force that shapes everything that happens in this incredible place. From the migration of animals to the growth of plants and even the way people live, the changing seasons determine the rhythm of life on these vast plains. The Serengeti's climate has created a delicate balance, one that has allowed countless species to thrive here for millions of years. By understanding how the climate works, we can better appreciate the beauty and complexity of the Serengeti and work to protect it in the face of a changing world.

Chapter 19: Nighttime Adventures in the Serengeti

As the sun sets over the Serengeti, the landscape undergoes a remarkable transformation. The vast plains, which are so familiar and full of life during the day, become a world of mystery and adventure as darkness falls. This is when the Serengeti's nocturnal creatures begin to emerge, and the night takes on a life of its own. For many animals, nighttime is their time to shine, and the Serengeti becomes a different place, full of sounds, sights, and secrets that most people never get to witness.

When the golden glow of the sun dips below the horizon, a hush falls over the land, but this quiet is quickly replaced by the calls and cries of animals preparing for the night ahead. Lions, which are known to rest for most of the day, become active hunters under the cover of darkness. These big cats are perfectly designed for nighttime adventures, with eyes that allow them to see in low light and muscles that are built for silent, powerful movements. As the temperature cools, lions take advantage of the cooler night air to stalk their prey, often moving in groups called prides. You can almost feel the tension in the air as they silently creep through the grass, their eyes locked on their next meal.

Lions aren't the only predators that thrive at night. Hyenas, those clever scavengers with their eerie laughs, come alive after dusk. While hyenas often get a bad reputation as scavengers that steal food from other animals, they are also skilled hunters. Their sharp senses help them find food in the dark, and their strong jaws can crush bones, allowing them to eat nearly every part of an animal. They roam in packs, communicating with each other through whoops and giggles that can send shivers down your spine. Despite their spooky sounds, hyenas play an important role in the Serengeti ecosystem by cleaning up the remains of dead animals, ensuring that nothing goes to waste.

Leopards are another predator that thrives under the cloak of night. These solitary cats are experts at remaining hidden, even in broad daylight, but at night, they use the darkness to their full advantage. Leopards are excellent climbers, and they often drag their prey up into trees to keep it safe from other predators like lions or hyenas. With their spotted coats blending into the shadows, they are nearly invisible as they move silently through the trees or along rocky outcrops. Leopards are elusive and rarely seen during the day, but nighttime is when they do most of their hunting, slipping through the darkness like ghosts.

The Serengeti's herbivores are not completely safe at night, but they have their own ways of surviving. Zebras, wildebeest, and antelope don't have the same night vision as predators, so they rely on their keen senses of hearing and smell to detect danger. Many of these animals sleep in groups, with some staying awake to keep watch while others rest. Their strategy is to stick together, hoping that the safety of numbers will protect them from being singled out by hungry predators. Even at night, the plains are full of movement as these animals shuffle nervously, aware that danger could be lurking in the darkness.

In the rivers, another set of nighttime adventures takes place. Crocodiles and hippos, both of which spend much of their day in the water to stay cool, become more active after dark. Hippos, despite their enormous size, leave the water at night to graze on grass. These seemingly slow and lazy animals can move surprisingly fast on land, covering great distances in search of food. While they may look gentle, hippos are actually quite dangerous and are known to be very protective of their territory. Crocodiles, on the other hand, remain near the water, using the darkness to ambush animals that come to the river's edge to drink. With their powerful jaws and stealthy movements, they are some of the most fearsome nighttime hunters in the Serengeti.

One of the most magical parts of the Serengeti at night is the sound. With fewer human-made noises and the quiet of the day behind them, the natural sounds of the Serengeti become even more noticeable. The hoots of owls, the chirps of crickets, and the distant roars of lions create a symphony of wilderness. Frogs croak in the water, and the rustling of leaves hints at small creatures moving through the underbrush. These nighttime sounds can be both comforting and eerie, reminding anyone listening that the Serengeti is alive, even in the darkest hours.

Insects also play a major role in the nighttime Serengeti. While they might not be as big or as famous as the lions or elephants, they are just as important. Moths and beetles flutter around in the cool night air, attracted to the moonlight. Termites, which build towering mounds across the plains, are often busy repairing their homes or foraging for food. And let's not forget about the mosquitoes, which are small but can be quite pesky. Bats swoop through the air, catching insects in mid-flight with their excellent echolocation skills. These tiny hunters may not be as fearsome as a lion, but they're just as impressive in their own way, using their senses to navigate through the dark and find food.

Nighttime in the Serengeti is also a time for some of the smaller, often overlooked animals to come out and explore. Creatures like porcupines, aardvarks, and genets are usually hidden during the day but take advantage of the cover of night to search for food. Porcupines, with their spiky quills, shuffle around looking for plants to eat, while aardvarks use their long snouts to sniff out termites and ants. Genets, small cat-like animals with long, bushy tails, dart through the grass, their large eyes glowing in the darkness as they hunt for insects and small rodents.

Another fascinating aspect of the Serengeti at night is the stars. Without the bright lights of cities, the sky above the Serengeti becomes a blanket of stars, stretching from horizon to horizon. The Milky Way, that shimmering band of light made up of billions of stars, is visible in all its glory. For the Maasai people, who have lived in the Serengeti for centuries, the stars have played an important role in their culture and traditions. They use the stars to navigate and to tell stories, passing down their knowledge of the night sky from generation to generation. Stargazing in the Serengeti is an experience unlike any other, where the vastness of the universe feels as close as the animals that roam the plains below.

Even though the Serengeti can seem peaceful at night, it's a place of constant movement and change. Rangers and conservationists, who work tirelessly to protect this incredible ecosystem, often conduct patrols at night to keep an eye on poachers and to monitor the health of the animals. These brave men and women face many challenges, but their dedication helps ensure that the animals of the Serengeti can continue to thrive. For them, the Serengeti at night is not just a place of adventure, but a place of responsibility, where every sound and movement might indicate an animal in need or a threat to the delicate balance of the ecosystem.

In recent years, more people have become interested in experiencing the Serengeti at night through guided night safaris. These safaris give visitors the chance to see animals they wouldn't normally see during the day, like the elusive leopards or the playful aardvarks. Equipped with special red lights that don't disturb the animals, safari guides help visitors explore the nocturnal side of the Serengeti. It's a completely different experience from a daytime safari—more mysterious, more thrilling, and filled with surprises around every corner.

In conclusion, nighttime in the Serengeti is a world of its own, full of adventures, dangers, and beauty that can only be experienced when the sun goes down. The animals of the Serengeti have adapted to life in the dark, and for many of them, it's the most important time of the day. From the powerful lions stalking through the grass to the tiny bats flitting through the sky, every creature has its role to play in the Serengeti's nighttime drama. And for those lucky enough to witness it, the Serengeti at night offers a glimpse into a side of nature that's as enchanting as it is wild.

Chapter 20: The Circle of Life in the Serengeti

In the vast and wild plains of the Serengeti, the "Circle of Life" is one of the most fascinating natural cycles that constantly unfolds before your eyes. This circle refers to the way that all living things, from the tiniest insects to the mightiest predators, are interconnected in a delicate balance of survival. Every plant, animal, and even the land itself plays a role in this incredible system, where life and death are part of the same eternal rhythm. The Serengeti, with its incredible diversity of wildlife, is a place where this cycle is easy to see, but understanding it requires looking closer at how each piece fits into the whole.

The Circle of Life in the Serengeti begins with the land, which is the foundation for everything else. The rich soil of the Serengeti's plains supports a wide variety of grasses and plants that cover the landscape. These grasses are not only beautiful as they sway in the wind, but they are also the primary food source for many of the Serengeti's herbivores. Animals like zebras, wildebeest, and gazelles spend their days grazing on these grasses, relying on the nutrients they provide to grow strong and stay healthy. Without the grass, these herbivores wouldn't survive, and in turn, many other creatures would struggle as well.

But it's not just the grass that's important—it's the rains that help the grass grow. The Serengeti has a very specific pattern of rainy and dry seasons, which dictate when the land becomes lush and green or when it dries out and turns golden. When the rains come, the plains come alive with new growth, providing a feast for the herbivores. These rains are part of the circle because they replenish the earth and allow the plants to flourish, which in turn supports the entire ecosystem. Without the rains, the cycle would break down, and life would become much more difficult for all the animals living here.

Herbivores, or plant-eating animals, are a major part of the Circle of Life in the Serengeti. Zebras, wildebeest, and other grazing animals spend their days moving across the plains in search of fresh grass. These animals are constantly on the move, following the rains in search of new pastures. While they eat, they also help to maintain the balance of the ecosystem by keeping the grass trimmed, which encourages new growth. Their droppings also fertilize the soil, helping the grass grow even stronger. This connection between the land and the animals is one of the reasons why the Serengeti is such a rich and vibrant place.

The herbivores are not just feeding themselves—they are also providing food for the Serengeti's predators. This is where the circle continues. Lions, cheetahs, leopards, and hyenas are all part of this system, and their survival depends on their ability to hunt and capture prey. Predators play a crucial role in the Circle of Life by keeping the herbivore populations in check. Without predators, herbivores would multiply too quickly and eat all the grass, leaving the land bare and causing the entire ecosystem to collapse. Predators ensure that the balance is maintained by removing the weak, the old, and the sick from the herbivore populations, allowing the strongest and healthiest animals to survive and reproduce.

Lions, often called the "kings of the Serengeti," are one of the most well-known predators in this circle. They are skilled hunters, usually working together in prides to take down larger prey like wildebeest or zebras. Their ability to hunt and catch prey is a key part of the Circle of Life because it ensures that their own families have enough food to survive, while also keeping the herbivore populations from growing too large. Cheetahs, known for their incredible speed, prefer smaller prey like gazelles. Each predator has a role to play, and they have all adapted to hunting in different ways that allow them to survive in the Serengeti's unique environment.

After a predator has made a kill, it's not only the big cats that benefit. Scavengers like hyenas and vultures also play a vital role in the Circle of Life. These animals may not always hunt for themselves, but they help clean up the remains of animals left behind by other predators. Hyenas, despite their reputation as scavengers, are actually very skilled hunters themselves, but they also take advantage of opportunities to feed on animals that have already been killed. Vultures are often the last to arrive at a carcass, but they are crucial to the ecosystem because they help dispose of the bones and other remains that might otherwise spread disease.

Even after all the scavengers have had their fill, the cycle continues. What's left of an animal's body will decompose, returning nutrients to the soil. This process is carried out by insects and microorganisms, which break down the remaining bones and flesh into organic matter that enriches the earth. These nutrients help new plants to grow, and the circle begins again. Without decomposition, the Serengeti's soil would eventually lose its fertility, and the plants would struggle to grow. This hidden part of the Circle of Life might not be as dramatic as a lion's hunt, but it's just as important.

Another important aspect of the Circle of Life in the Serengeti is reproduction. Every year, during the Great Migration, millions of wildebeest, zebras, and gazelles journey across the Serengeti in search of fresh grass. Along the way, many animals give birth to their young, ensuring that the next generation is ready to take their place in the circle. The survival of these young animals is crucial because they represent the future of their species. Many young herbivores fall prey to predators, but enough survive to grow up and continue the cycle. This constant renewal of life is what keeps the Serengeti thriving year after year.

The Serengeti's elephants are another important part of this cycle. As the largest land animals, they have a huge impact on their environment. Elephants spend much of their time feeding on trees and shrubs, which helps to shape the landscape. By knocking down trees and trampling vegetation, they create open spaces that allow grass to grow, benefiting the herbivores. Elephants also dig for water in dry riverbeds, creating waterholes that other animals can use. Their role as ecosystem engineers makes them a critical part of the Circle of Life, and their presence helps to maintain the balance of the Serengeti's environment.

The role of water in the Circle of Life cannot be underestimated. During the dry season, water becomes scarce, and animals must travel long distances to find it. Rivers, lakes, and waterholes become gathering places for animals of all kinds. Hippos spend their days in the water to keep cool, while crocodiles lurk just beneath the surface, waiting for unsuspecting prey. Fish, frogs, and other aquatic creatures also depend on these water sources. Without water, life in the Serengeti would be impossible. The arrival of the rains each year not only replenishes the land but also renews the water sources, ensuring that the cycle can continue.

One of the most remarkable things about the Circle of Life in the Serengeti is how resilient it is. Even when challenges arise, such as droughts, disease, or human interference, the animals and plants of the Serengeti find ways to adapt and survive. This adaptability is what has allowed the Serengeti to remain one of the most important ecosystems in the world, despite the many changes it has faced over time. Conservation efforts by rangers and scientists help to protect this delicate balance, ensuring that the Circle of Life continues for future generations.

At the heart of the Circle of Life is the idea that every creature, no matter how big or small, plays a role in the Serengeti's ecosystem. From the tiniest insects that pollinate plants to the powerful predators that rule the plains, each animal contributes to the survival of the whole system. This interconnectedness is what makes the Serengeti such a special place, where life is constantly renewing itself and every day brings new stories of survival, birth, and growth.

In conclusion, the Circle of Life in the Serengeti is a never-ending cycle that connects all living things. It begins with the land and the rain, which nourish the plants, which in turn feed the herbivores. The herbivores support the predators, and the predators, along with scavengers, help maintain the balance of the ecosystem. When life ends, it nourishes the earth, and new life begins again. The Serengeti is a place where this cycle is constantly in motion, reminding us that life and death are part of the same natural rhythm, and that every living thing has a role to play in this magnificent web of life.

Epilogue

You've reached the end of our journey through the magnificent Serengeti, but the adventure doesn't stop here! As you've discovered, the Serengeti is more than just a place—it's a living, breathing world where animals roam free, seasons change, and life never stands still. From the sweeping migrations of wildebeest to the quiet strength of the Maasai people, the Serengeti shows us the beauty and power of nature in every moment.

Now that you know about the amazing creatures, landscapes, and wonders of this wild paradise, you have a deeper understanding of how important it is to protect places like the Serengeti. Every animal, from the tiniest insect to the largest elephant, plays a part in keeping the balance of this magical ecosystem.

As you close this book, remember that the Serengeti is just one of many incredible places on Earth that need our care. Whether you dream of visiting one day or simply want to learn more about our planet's wild wonders, your adventure is only just beginning. The Serengeti will always be here, waiting for new explorers like you to discover its endless stories. Keep exploring, keep learning, and never stop being amazed by the natural world!

The End.

www.ingramcontent.com/pod-product-compliance
Lightning Source LLC
Chambersburg PA
CBHW031433130726
47989CB00003B/1123